ZOMBIES A-Z

D A N   O L I V E R

JOHN BLAKE

Published by John Blake Publishing Ltd,
3 Bramber Court, 2 Bramber Road,
London W14 9PB, England

www.johnblakepublishing.co.uk

www.facebook.com/Johnblakepub `facebook`
twitter.com/johnblakepub `twitter`

First published in paperback in 2011

ISBN: 978-1-84358-638-8

British Library Cataloguing-in-Publication Data:

A catalogue record for this book is available from the British Library.

Design by www.envydesign.co.uk

Printed and bound by CPI Group (UK) Ltd, Croydon, CR0 4YY

1 3 5 7 9 10 8 6 4 2

Papers used by John Blake Publishing are natural, recyclable products
made from wood grown in sustainable forests. The manufacturing processes
conform to the environmental regulations of the country of origin.

Every attempt has been made to contact the relevant copyright-holders,
but some were unobtainable. We would be grateful if the appropriate
people could contact us.

Dedicated to zombie superfans Victoria Pointon, Eloise Rowe and Mark Henderson. A special thank you to Matthew Richardson and Mike Dodgson, authors of *The Inbetweeners A–Z*.

A IS FOR....

ALIEN DEAD (1980)

Alien Dead is a horror movie directed by Fred Olen Ray, who also wrote the screenplay with the help of Martin Nicholas. Fred is best known for his work on the TV show *The Lair* and for directing *Evil Toons* and *Scalps*. He cast Buster Crabbe as Sheriff Kowalski, Ray Roberts as Tom, Linda Lewis as Shawn and George Kelsey as Emmet.

The tranquil peace and quiet in a sleepy American town is broken when a meteor strikes and hits a houseboat. The occupants of the houseboat become zombies and need to feed in order to survive. At first they eat the alligators that live in the swamp, but soon they start eating humans when they run out of alligators. They kidnap people from the town and eat them, but do it in secret so no one knows that they are zombies. As more and more people start disappearing, the local scientist grows suspicious and decides to investigate.

ARMY OF DARKNESS (1992)

The third movie in the Evil Dead trilogy, *Army of Darkness* is a slapstick comedy horror movie, which sets it apart from the first two movies. In it, Ash is trapped in medieval England and has to fight the zombies — called deadites — to reach the present day. The movie was directed by Sam Raimi, who wrote it with his brother Ivan. It stars Bruce Campbell as Ashley J 'Ash' Williams, Embeth Davidtz as Sheila and Marcus Gilbert as Lord Arthur.

In the movie, Ash and his girlfriend Linda find the Book of the Dead and open it. Linda is killed by the satanic force it unleashes. Ash is forced to chainsaw his hand off when the force enters him and it ends up sending him to the Dark Ages along with his Oldsmobile, chainsaw and shotgun.

Ash is captured by Lord Arthur's men who strip him of his weapons because they think he has been working for Duke Henry, their enemy. He is taken to the castle with Duke Henry's men and is thrown in the Pit of Death, which contains deadites. It looks like Ash could be about to die but then the Wise Man tosses him his chainsaw. Once he has destroyed a deadite, he climbs out of the pit and gets his gun back.

He manages to get Henry released, which makes him a hero in people's eyes. Ash falls for a woman called Sheila, whose brother is one of Arthur's knights, but still wants to get home. He finds out from the Wise Man that he needs a special book called the *Necronomicon*.

Ash sets out and travels through a haunted forest. He is chased by something and hides in a windmill but manages to break a mirror. Things get a bit strange when his reflections climb out of the pieces of mirror and start taunting him. One manages to get inside him by diving down his throat and becomes a life-size copy of him, but Ash manages to kill and bury it.

He continues on his quest but when he arrives at the location of the *Necronomicon* he finds three books instead of the one he was expecting. He manages to distinguish which is the real book but when it comes to reciting 'Klaatu barada nikto' so he can take the book safely he can't. He remembers the first two words but can't remember the last one so he mumbles it, thinking that he can get away with it. Big mistake.

Ash takes the book and quickly returns to the castle. But because he didn't remember the last word he has awoken the dead, who start coming up from their graves — even his life-size copy. The deadites join the Army of Darkness and Sheila is taken by a deadite. Ash wants to go home but he can't — he has to help put things right. He wants to lead the people against the army led by his life-size copy, but they aren't sure about it. He uses some textbooks to learn what they need to do and Duke Henry helps him. They manage to defeat Ash's life-size copy and the army before Ash goes back to the future thanks to a special potion from the *Necronomicon*.

Ash tells a colleague in the S-Mart store what he has been up to and that he could have been a medieval king if he had wanted. He manages to mess things up again when he causes a demon to possess one of the female workers, but he manages to kill it and then kisses the woman. The voice-over declares: 'Sure, I could have stayed in the past. Could have even been king. But in my own way, I am king.'

The movie might have been set in medieval England but it was filmed in California, in the Bronson Canyon and Vasquez Rocks Natural Area Park. They built the castle on the edge of the Mojave Desert and the interior scenes were shot in Hollywood. The script was written while Sam and Ivan were producing the movie *Darkman*, an action superhero movie that Sam wrote and directed. They had been given an initial budget of $8 million but this wasn't enough to do the script justice because of the special effects needed. Happily *Darkman* was a success, so Universal Pictures agreed to fund half of the movie's budget and Sam, Bruce Campbell and Rob Tapert, the movie's producers, each gave some of their salary. They still couldn't do exactly what they had wanted to do, but that couldn't be helped.

After the movie had been finished Universal decided that they didn't like the ending, which was deemed too negative. The company wanted one where Ash was a hero, so a new one was filmed. The company also cut some scenes – including one where a deadite was decapitated – after the movie was given an NC-17 rating, which meant that no children under 17 could see it, and the company wanted it to be suitable for all. It ended up with an R rating, which meant that anyone could see it, as long as children were accompanied by an adult.

Generally, *Army of Darkness* got good reviews. It was given a score of 71 out of 100 (based on 88 reviews) by the website Rotten Tomatoes, although this wasn't as high as the previous two Evil Dead movies, which received scores of 100 and 98.

Critics did enjoy the movie, however. Desson Howe from *The Washington Post* wrote in his review: 'There's a little Monty Python black humor at work here. There are moments of cyberpunkish mutation. You'll also find remnants of Arthurian legend, *Gulliver's Travels* and, uh, the Three Stooges. But the movie has an original life of its own.

'Bill Pope's cinematography is gymnastic and appropriately frenetic. The visual and make-up effects (from artist-technicians William Mesa, Tony Gardner and others) are incredibly imaginative. Ash contends with even more Books of the Dead that suck him into nightmarish hells. He has run-ins with teeth-clattering, scary skeletons that recall the great old Ray Harryhausen movies.'

Owen Gleiberman in *Entertainment Weekly* gave the movie only a C+ rating but still liked the movie, writing: 'The director sends his usual hero, the square-jawed wiseacre Ash (Bruce Campbell), through a time warp and back to the Dark Ages, where he comes on like a smart-ass cross between Indiana Jones and Mad Max. With his Dudley Do-Right chin and light-as-air machismo, Campbell is a walking human cartoon, and it's fun to watch him drop insults in late-20th-century slang and treat his medieval hosts, including the demons, with brazen contempt ("Yo, she-bitch, let's go!").

'There are also a few flashes of Raimi at his best: a loony-tunes sequence in which Ash does bloody battle with Lilliputian versions of himself, an encounter with the Book of the Dead that leaves his face all bent out of shape. As always, Raimi's "evil dead" are amusingly corporeal: in *Army of Darkness*, the rubber-faced ghouls and witchy-poos don't just spook you – they thwack you in the face.'

Army of Darkness was a big hit in the cinema and made $21.5 million. Fans loved the movie and it was nominated for a host of awards. At the Saturn Awards it won for Best Horror Film and was nominated for Best Make-Up, but lost out to *Interview with the Vampire*. It won the Critics' Award at Fantasporto and the Golden Raven Award at the Brussels International Festival of Fantasy Film. It also received nominations for the Grand Prize at the Avoriaz Fantastic Film Festival, Best Film at the International Fantasy Film Awards and Best Film at the Spanish International Film Festival.

TOP THREE QUOTES

Ash: 'You see this? THIS… is my BOOMSTICK'

Sheila: 'You found me beautiful once.'
Ash: 'Honey, you got real ugly.'

Arthur: 'Are all men from the future loud-mouthed braggarts?'
Ash: 'Nope. Just me baby… Just me.'

DID YOU KNOW?

'Klaatu barada nikto' is a line from the movie *The Day the Earth Stood Still*. No official translation has ever been given.

The original ending had Ash sitting in a cave in his Oldsmobile, drinking a potion given to him by a Merlin-like figure. He drinks too much and grows a huge beard, and ends up waking up after an apocalypse.

If you love Evil Dead movies, check out the website Deadites Online (www.deadites.net) to find out the latest news and meet other fans of the trilogy in the forum. You can also hunt down back issues of several comic series featuring the Evil Dead characters and storylines.

AUTOMATON TRANSFUSION (2006)

A horror movie directed and written by Steven C Miller, *Automaton Transfusion* was released as the first in a trilogy. (*Automaton Transfusion 2* is due to be released in 2012.) The movie stars Garrett Jones as Chris, Juliet Reeves as Jackie, William Howard Bowman as Scott and Rowan Bousaid as Tim.

The movie follows what happens to three best friends during a zombie attack. Scott, Chris and Tim decide to go out and watch a band in a bar. On the way there they wonder why there are no cars on the road and why they can't see anyone. It's rush hour so the roads should be packed. When they arrive at the bar they are chased by a group of zombies and have to fight for their lives.

It turns out that the US government is to blame, as back in the 1970s they wanted to find a way of bringing the dead back to life. They have recently reopened the project, but in doing so have caused a zombie apocalypse.

DID YOU KNOW?

Automaton Transfusion was awarded third place in the Best Feature Independent Feature Film category at the Toronto After Dark Spirit Awards.

B IS FOR...

BENEATH STILL WATERS (2005)

Directed by Brian Yuzna, *Beneath Still Waters* brings us zombies and the supernatural against a backdrop of a Spanish town. It stars Michael McKell, Raquel Meroño and Charlotte Salt.

The town is due to celebrate its 400th anniversary, but history has a hold on the sleepy place and the celebrations are destined for terror. Four hundred years earlier, the leaders of the town flooded a nearby village, leaving Satan-worshippers chained inside the local church, thus burying them forever under water... or so they hoped. But what they hadn't planned for all those years ago was two teens deciding to take a look around the doomed village and getting trapped as it flooded.

In the present day, the townspeople are preparing for the celebrations when a local boy goes missing while swimming with his girlfriend. The ancient village is behind the boy's death, but it's left to a newbie reporter and diver to solve the mysteries of the zombie village and its victims.

DID YOU KNOW?

Beneath Still Waters is based on the novel of the same title by Matthew J Costello.

THE BEYOND (1981)

An Italian zombie movie, *The Beyond* was directed by Lucio Fulci, and is the second in the Gates of Hell trilogy. A blood-filled horror-fest, it has gained cult status with horror fans despite being heavily censored because of its extremely gory scenes.

The story follows Liza Merril (Catriona MacColl), who has arrived in New Orleans from New York to claim her inheritance of a hotel out in the swamps of Louisiana. But what she doesn't know is that, years earlier, the cellar of the Seven Doors hotel was the scene of the gruesome lynching of an artist called Schweik, who was believed to be a warlock. The torture consisted of a beating, a dousing with acid and a crucifixion, despite warnings by the artist that he would unleash evil on the attackers.

The hotel is creepy from the outset. The spooky servants, Arthur (Gianpaolo Saccarola) and Martha (Veronica Lazar), look otherworldly. It's not long after Liza starts her renovation that strange things begin to happen. The first victim is a painter working on the building, who suffers serious injuries when he falls off his rig. Coughing up blood and speaking in tongues, he starts speaking of 'the eyes', but no one knows what he's talking about. It's not long before another workman falls victim to the hotel. This time it's a plumber, Joe, who, when trying to repair a leak in the cellar, is murdered by a mysterious creature after he opens up a hole to the supernatural underworld. The body is discovered by the creepy Martha near the corpse of the warlock artist, Schweik.

The spookiness continues when Liza finds a blind woman called Emily wandering down an empty highway. She tells Liza that she's been waiting for her, and that she must leave the hotel while she still can.

Meanwhile, at the morgue, Joe's wife Mary-Ann has arrived to prepare her husband's body for the funeral, when she is burned with acid and murdered. Her daughter is then attacked by Schweik's corpse after Dr

John McCabe's assistant, Harris, inserts an EMG machine into the body to measure electrical activity in its muscles.

Liza tells Dr McCabe of her worries about the strange goings-on in the hotel, including the weird staff. He tells her he's never heard of either of them, and he knows the people of the area well. The two then find out about the death of Joe's wife, and that her daughter was found petrified in the morgue, too scared to talk. After Liza goes to their funeral, she is again warned by Emily about the paranormal activity at the hotel. Emily tells Liza about the dead artist, about room 36 where he stayed, and about a supernatural underworld the hotel conceals. Suddenly Emily is scared by one of Schweik's paintings, and rushes out of the hotel. Liza notices that she floats above the floor.

Liza decides to confront her fears of the hotel. She takes a look around the supposedly haunted room 36, where she finds a skin-covered book called *Eibon*, and Schweik's corpse nailed to the wall of the bathroom! She runs to John McCabe, who goes back into the room, to find only two nails in the wall. He then tells the frightened Liza that there is no woman called Emily living where she describes.

John decides to investigate Emily's house, but when he goes to the area Liza tells him about, he finds an old derelict building, with nothing inside apart from the book *Eibon*.

Meanwhile, Liza goes for a walk with Martin Avery and she sees a copy of *Eibon* in a bookshop's window, but when she goes inside the book has disappeared. Martin goes alone to the local library to find the blueprints of the hotel but dark forces knock him off his ladder as he searches. He breaks his neck and huge supernatural tarantulas eat his face.

Back at the hotel, Arthur is killed as he tries to close the hole in the cellar's wall and a zombie of Joe the plumber appears when Martha is cleaning room 36. She is impaled on a nail in the bathroom. The next victim is Emily. Back at her house – which is once again filled with expensive furniture – zombies of Arthur, Joe, Mary-Ann and Schweik appear to force Emily back to hell. She doesn't want to go and sets her guide dog Dickie on Schweik, but the dog turns on her and rips her throat out.

On his return to the hotel, John rescues Liza and reveals to her that the hotel is one of the seven gateways to hell. As he speaks the flooded cellar becomes overrun with the undead, as the gates have opened. John and Liza manage to escape, only to find the city desolate. The pair head to the hospital so John can get his gun. They encounter gangs of zombies and John finds Harris, but his colleague is killed when a window shatters and the glass impales him against the hospital wall.

Forced into the morgue by the zombies, John and

Liza join Joe's daughter Jill and start to fight the zombies off. Suddenly Jill turns on them and it appears that, like Emily, she is working for the dark forces. John shoots her but then is forced downstairs with Liza by the corpse of Schweik.

Unbelievably they find themselves back in the cellar of the spooky hotel, where they walk through a hole in the wall and find themselves in one of Schweik's paintings, trapped forever in the land of the undead!

DID YOU KNOW?

The director Lucio Fulci makes an appearance in the film as a strange librarian.

BEYOND RE-ANIMATOR (2003)

The third movie in the Re-Animator series, and the second directed by Brian Yuzna, *Beyond Re-Animator* catches up with Dr Herbert West, 13 years into his prison sentence following the death of a girl in one of his zombie experiments.

Despite his incarceration, Herbert (Jeffrey Combs) has been continuing with his experiments, performing them on rats in the prison. He believes the experiments, although basic, have unearthed what was missing in his earlier reanimation process, and he starts working with a young doctor, Howard Phillips (Jason Barry). The missing link in Herbert's earlier experiments is nano-plasmic energy – the energy released at the moment of death – and the mad doctor has managed to store this energy in capsules through his continued work.

When the prison warden (Simón Andreu) finds out what Herbert and Howard are up to, the two doctors kill him. Herbert then uses the nano-plasmic energy from a rat to reanimate the warden, creating a human-looking zombie with the tendencies of a rat! As a result the prison turns to chaos as the inmates get their hands on Herbert's reagent, until it becomes hard to distinguish the dead from the living.

Again, Herbert seems to escape most of the madness, leaving his new sidekick weeping over the severed head of his girlfriend, and managing to get out of the prison as the movie closes.

DID YOU KNOW?

Howard Phillips – the name of Herbert's new colleague – are the first names of HP Lovecraft, who wrote the original story on which this movie was based.

THE BONEYARD (1991)

Directed by James Cummins, *The Boneyard* went straight to video. It combines gory horror, comedy and sarcasm, making for a very individual movie.

The movie revolves around Alley Cates (Deborah Rose), a down-and-out psychic, suffering from depression, who is hired by police officers Jersey Callum and Gordon Mullen to help in their investigation into the murder of three kids. The prime suspect for the killing is Chen (Robert Yun Ju Ahn), a mortician and funeral home owner. The bodies of the children contained other human remains, apparently force-fed to them before death.

Hoping to find out what actually happened to the victims, Alley accompanies the officers to the coroner's office, where they meet Miss Poopinplatz (Phyllis Diller) and Shepard, the mortuary attendant. When Alley tries to uncover the circumstances of the deaths by holding locks of the hair from one of the corpses, she is struck by a vision of the three corpses rising from the dead. She realises that this is actually happening and rushes upstairs to warn the officers who are with the bodies, but they're gone... and the room is splattered with blood.

The psychic then has her beliefs fully realised when she catches the three corpses feasting on other dead bodies. She runs from the flesh-hungry kids as the weird and wacky Miss Poopinplatz comes to investigate, pet poodle in tow. Madness follows. Miss Poopinplatz is turned into a zombie, and her poodle is also transformed into a giant zombie in one of the funniest and most random twists to a zombie movie ever.

BRAINDEAD/DEAD ALIVE (1992)

Produced and filmed in New Zealand under the direction of Peter Jackson – most famous for later directing The Lord of the Rings trilogy, *King Kong* and *The Hobbit* – *Braindead* combines comedy and horror and a whole lot more, and is one of the goriest films ever made. Despite censorship in the US, the movie achieved considerable recognition, receiving Best Director, Best Film and Best Screenplay at the New Zealand Film and TV Awards and the Silver Scream Award at the Amsterdam Fantastic Film Festival.

The movie opens with an explorer returning from an expedition from the ominously named Skull Island, carrying a rat-monkey in a cage. According to legend, this cross-species was created when a plague of rats raped monkeys on the mysterious island. The explorer and his guide are stopped in their tracks by native warriors, who order him to return the monkey. When he refuses and tries to escape, he is bitten by the hybrid monkey, leading his men to first cut off his arm and then kill him – shipping the monkey to Wellington Zoo, New Zealand.

We then meet Lionel Cosgrove and his mum. She is so angry about his relationship with a woman called Paquita that she follows the pair to the zoo, but while there she is bitten by the rat-monkey and transforms into a zombie. Still, her son doesn't abandon her and tries to take care of his zombie mum, but when she starts killing other people he decides enough is enough and tranquilises her. She escapes and is hit by a tram but doesn't die because she is a zombie. So that no one suspects anything, Lionel holds a fake funeral.

Unfortunately for Lionel, six feet of dirt isn't enough to hold his mother and she escapes before he can tranquilise her again. She kills more people, bringing more zombies and violence to the New Zealand town. He continues trying to keep this escalating mess under control, tranquilising the zombies and keeping them at his house. When his uncle Les discovers the bodies, he blackmails Lionel into giving him his inheritance.

Lionel again decides enough is enough and issues the zombies with poison to kill them once and for all. But instead of giving them a lethal injection, he feeds them a stimulant, and they start attacking guests at his housewarming party!

The movie ends with Lionel, Paquita and Les all fighting an army of zombies. Lionel and Paquita survive, killing all the zombies except for Lionel's mother. Now a huge monster, she traps the pair, grabs her son and throws him into her womb before giving birth to him again. This has got to be one of the weirdest scenes in any zombie movie, but, thankfully for Lionel, he cuts the monster on his way out of her womb and she finally dies. This leaves the happy couple to live the rest of their lives together, and the film closes with the pair arm in arm (covered in blood).

DID YOU KNOW?

The location used to shoot Skull Island was later re-used by Jackson in *The Lord of the Rings: The Return of the King* as the location of the Paths of the Dead.

BRIDE OF RE-ANIMATOR (1990)

Written and directed by Brian Yuzna, the second movie in the Re-Animator series continues the story almost a year after the first film. Dr Herbert West (Jeffrey Combs) and Dr Dan Cain (Bruce Abbott) now find themselves working as medics in the middle of the Peruvian civil war – evidently a great location to continue their experiments!

After their medical tent is stormed by enemy troops, the two men return home. They pick up work as doctors at the local hospital, but the real work takes place in their lab in the basement of Dan's house. This time, instead of trying to reanimate one corpse, the pair use stolen body parts from the morgue and plan to build Dan a new Meg, using his girlfriend's heart.

At the morgue, the pathologist Wilbur Graves finds the head of Dr Carl Hill from the first movie, along with some of Herbert's reagent. He decides to perform his own experiment with the solution, and brings the severed head back to life… again.

The events of the first movie are not forgotten in the sequel. The local police officer, Lt Leslie Chapham, is suspicious of the two doctors, believing it was they who were responsible for the outbreak of zombies, of which his wife was one. His investigations lead the officer to the secret lab, filled with dead bodies and body parts. When he questions Herbert about this discovery, Herbert attacks and kills him, then brings his body back to life as a zombie to cover up the murder.

The zombified policeman is taken under the control of the severed head of Carl, who commands him to sew bat wings onto the side of his head so he can move again. The now mobile Carl has control over Chapham and the last remaining zombies from the first film… Herbert and Dan had better watch out!

With his army of zombies, Carl arrives at the house

of Herbert and Dan as the final stages of the reincarnation of the zombie bride Meg are taking place. A mêlée of attacks follows at the house, now filled with zombies, severed heads, mad scientists and more. The first clash is between the Frankenstein monster-like bride and Dan's new girlfriend, leading to the zombie tearing her own heart out after Dan sides with his living girlfriend, Francesca.

Carl and his army of zombies now attack Herbert, Dan and Francesca, forcing them out of the house through an underground wall to a tomb in the graveyard next door. More body parts start coming back to life, and as the crypt suddenly collapses, only Dan and Francesca seem to make it out alive.

DID YOU KNOW?

The movie was nominated for the Saturn Award for Best Horror Film and the Saturn Award for Best Supporting Actor (Jeffrey Combs) by the Academy of Science Fiction, Fantasy and Horror Films.

C IS FOR...

THE CABINET OF DR CALIGARI (1920)

One of the first horror films to feature a zombie, *The Cabinet of Dr Caligari* was a German silent horror film directed by Robert Wiene. The screenplay was written by Carl Mayer and Hans Janowitz, and it was the first movie to have a twist at the end.

The plot tells the story of Dr Caligari (Werner Krauss) and his sleepwalking zombie Cesare (Conrad Veidt) who come to a German town as part of a carnival. The narrator, a man called Francis (Friedrich Feher), tells the story through a flashback. He visits the carnival with his friend Alan, and the two men go to see

Cesare, who is one of the attractions. People can ask Cesare anything they want and the psychic zombie will give them the correct answer. Alan asks him how long he has left to live and Cesare tells him he will die before dawn the next day.

When Alan does indeed die in the night, Francis is suspicious and wants to find out about Dr Caligari and Cesare. He takes his fiancée Jane with him to investigate but she ends up being kidnapped by Cesare. Dr Caligari wants her out of the way but Cesare won't kill her because she is so beautiful. He carries her away but he is chased by the people from the village and ends up dying of exhaustion.

Dr Caligari, meanwhile, has fled. Francis finds out that he is the director of an asylum and is obsessed by the story of a monk who, back in 1093, went by the name of Caligari and went on a murder spree using a sleepwalking creature he controlled. When Dr Caligari is confronted with Cesare's dead body, he shows everyone how crazed he is and ends up being imprisoned in his own asylum.

The twist at the end is that the story isn't a flashback – it is actually Francis's fantasy and he is a patient of the asylum, along with Jane and Cesare. Their doctor is Dr Caligari, and, after a scuffle with Francis, the doctor – now aware of the source of Francis's delusion – says he will be able to cure him.

Several adaptations of *The Cabinet of Dr Caligari* have

been made over the years and many modern-day movies and TV programmes have drawn on parts of the story. The 2009 movie *The Imaginarium of Doctor Parnassus* was also influenced by it, as was Superman's Metropolis series of graphic novels. In the cartoon series *Count Duckula*, the episode 'The Zombie Awakes' has a mad psychologist and a sleepwalking creature, and the overall look of the castle is in keeping with the distorted shadows and shapes in the silent movie.

CAMPBELL, BRUCE

Bruce Campbell is an American actor best known for playing Ash in the Evil Dead movies. He also played the lead roles in the TV series *The Adventures of Brisco County Jr* and *Jack of All Trades*. He has continued to work with Evil Dead director Sam Raimi, and has had cameos in three Spider-Man movies and in the 1990 movie *Darkman*.

Bruce is also a director, producer and writer, but he is most famous for being a B-movie actor. He gave his 2002 autobiography the title *If Chins Could Kill: Confessions of a B Movie Actor*. It became a *New York Times* bestseller. He also released a novel called *Make Love! The Bruce Campbell Way*.

Bruce started acting when he was a teenager at Wylie E Groves High School in Beverly Hills, Michigan – the same school that Sam Raimi went to. The pair started making Super 8 movies together with their friends while they were at the school. Bruce recalled to IGN how they met: 'I was born in the same hospital as Sam Raimi – the William Beaumont Hospital in Royal Oak. I met Sam in junior high – very briefly while I was with a friend of his – and he was dressed as Sherlock Holmes, playing with dolls. I thought he was a creepy weirdo and I avoided him, officially, until drama class in high school, in 1975. Sam was very much into magic, and I was his assistant at a couple of magic shows. Then I think Sam made a logical transition into film, being the ultimate sleight of hand.

'I think he started doing home movies in the early '70s. I did them in the early '70s, and we started making [them] – then I met other guys in our neighbourhood who had been making Super 8 movies longer than us, Scott Spiegel being one of them…. Josh Becker, who was Sam's neighbour… so there was a weird group of about six of us, who wound up teaming up and making Super 8 movies on weekends – almost every weekend.'

Bruce went to Western Michigan University to learn more about acting but still maintained his friendship with Sam. Together they filmed *Within the Woods*, which was a 30-minute version of *The Evil Dead*. They wanted people to like it in order to get the full movie financed. It worked and they set about filming *The Evil Dead* together with the producer Rob Tapert. It was a proper team effort and Bruce and Sam got their friends and family to help. Bruce might have been playing the leading man, Ash, but he also helped behind the camera too. Things really took off when they got the support of horror novelist Stephen King.

It took time for the movie to be distributed and it was four years before it made it to the UK. It became the number one movie in the UK and was a big hit in the US too. The first and second Evil Dead movies took horror films in a new direction and Bruce gained thousands of fans overnight. He had had no idea how big the Evil Dead movies would become or that he would be in the Marvel Zombies comics. (Ash was in five comics in the Marvel Zombies vs Army of Darkness series.)

In 2007 the movie *My Name is Bruce* was released, a comedy in which he plays a washed-up version of himself who is mistaken for his character Ash and has to take on a demon in a small mining town in Oregon. Sam Raimi also appears in three different roles. Bruce directed the movie, which is full of references to his other films.

CHILDREN OF THE LIVING DEAD (2001)

Directed by Tor Ramsey and written by Karen L Wolf, *Children of the Living Dead* was part of John A Russo's alternate Night of the Living Dead series. It was intended as a sequel to the 30th Anniversary Edition of *Night of the Living Dead*, but was made without director George A Romero.

The movie stars Tom Savini as Deputy Hughs, Martin Schiff as Deputy Randolph, Damien Luvara as Matthew Michaels and Jamie McCoy as Laurie Danesi. The story starts by looking back at a serial murderer and rapist called Abbott Hayes, whose corpse disappeared from a morgue during a zombie attack. Reanimated, he was even more bloodthirsty than he had been when alive. After taking control of the zombie attackers, he led them to ambush the town, killing everyone who crossed their path, before they were finally defeated and their bodies buried.

Fourteen years have passed and the town's residents are trying to forget what happened. A businessman arrives in town and decides to move the bodies from the zombie attack so he can build a car dealership. This is a huge mistake and soon the town has to deal with an angry Abbott Hayes and an army of zombies.

Critics and fans were disappointed with the movie. Walter Chaw from the Film Freak Central website wrote in his review: 'With the appearance of having been shot over a long weekend in someone's backyard, *Children of the Living Dead* is a cynical attempt to cash in on George A Romero's zombie trilogy (and *The Blair Witch Project*) so stale and amateurish that it qualifies as a barely releasable embarrassment to everyone involved, including gore-legend Tom Savini, who seems to have hit rock bottom in his extended cameo.'

Alex Sandell from the movie review website Juicy Cerebellum wasn't impressed either, writing: 'Pretty lame, but entertaining cheese, if you're in the mood.'

CITY OF THE LIVING DEAD (1980)

The first film in Italian director Lucio Fulci's unofficial Gates of Hell trilogy, *City of the Living Dead* stars Catriona MacColl as Mary, Fabrizio Jovine as Father Thomas and Christopher George as Peter.

Set in New York, the movie starts at a séance in the apartment of a medium named Theresa, but, as you might expect, things don't all go to plan. One of the people at the séance, Mary Woodhouse, suddenly starts shaking violently as she gets visions of a priest, Father Thomas, hanging himself in the cemetery of the New England village of Dunwich. Mary dies from these violent convulsions and the mystery begins...

The death of Mary brings a police investigation and interest from a journalist called Peter Bell. Theresa is questioned about the event as part of Sergeant Clay's investigation and she warns him that evil is afoot.

The following day is Mary's funeral, and she's buried

in a local cemetery. Peter is visiting Mary's grave (only half filled in by gravediggers), when he hears screaming as if from inside the coffin. He breaks open the casket, freeing Mary, and the pair return to Theresa. She warns them that Mary's visions of the dead priest are a sign that the door between this world and that of the undead is about to open, as the ancient book *Enoch* prophesises. She says that Father Thomas's death is responsible for this and that on All Saints Day the doors will open.

In the village of Dunwich, where Mary's vision was set, strange things start to happen. A teenager finds a rotting baby's corpse, while two other locals witness a mirror smashing of its own accord and unexplained cracks in walls. Several locals see the dead Father Thomas, covered in maggots. One girl who sees the dead priest is overcome by a powerful stare, causing her eyes to bleed and making her vomit her intestines out of her mouth, while her boyfriend has his head ripped off!

The strange goings-on get worse as All Saints Day approaches, with more visions of the dead Father Thomas, an attack by a corpse on a mortician, a visit from a dead girl called Emily who was smothered by the dead Father Thomas, bleeding walls and another gory murder. Peter and Mary manage to find the village from her visions and immediately head to the cemetery, where they search for the priest's tomb. They meet a couple, Gerry and Sandra, who have been subjected to the weird goings-on in the village. There are vicious attacks by the zombie Emily and Sandra has her head ripped off by the undead. Gerry also gets attacked by zombies, but manages to escape.

The death toll in the town quickly starts to rise and a state of emergency is declared over the radio. Mary, Peter and Gerry decide to return to the tomb of Father Thomas, where they find an underground cave filled with human remains. They are then attacked by the now zombified Sandra, who tears Peter's brains straight from his head. Gerry stabs her in the chest with a pitchfork and they are then confronted by the priest at the centre of all this. Father Thomas summons more dead from their tombs, but Gerry manages to attack him, tearing out his guts with a crucifix. This saves them, as by stopping the priest, the other zombies burst into flames and turn to dust, and the gates of hell are closed.

The movie ends with Emily's little brother running over to the pair as if to celebrate the saving of the town, but their faces turn to fear and the film ends as it started, with a scream from Mary, suggesting all is not yet well...

> **DID YOU KNOW?**
>
> The director of the film, Lucio Fulci, makes a cameo appearance as Dr Joe Thompson, the pathologist who discovers that Emily died from a heart attack brought on by fear.

COLIN (2008)

Most zombie movies cost millions to make, but not Marc Price's *Colin*. An English zombie movie, it cost only around £40 to make and was shot using a Panasonic Mini-DV camcorder over an 18-month period and edited using Adobe Premiere software. The people playing the zombies were recruited using Facebook and MySpace. In all, 100 actors were used and they played numerous roles, making do with whatever costumes and make-up they could find. They even had to bring their own lights and props. 'One of our make-up people came off *X-Men 3*,' Marc told CNN, 'so we were having the same latex that was put on Wolverine.'

Colin was the first movie to tell the entire story from a zombie's point of view, as the main character transforms into a zombie at the start of the movie. Marc revealed how the idea for Colin came to him: 'A couple of friends were round a few years ago watching Romero's *Dawn of the Dead* … and I wondered if a zombie movie from a zombie's perspective had been done before.'

In the movie Colin is attacked by his friend Damien, who is a zombie. Even though Colin manages to stab him to death, he turns into a zombie because of injuries he sustained earlier. He goes outside and walks alongside the other zombies. He wants human flesh and while he is being robbed for his trainers, he is spotted by his sister Linda, who is still human.

Colin goes on the hunt at a house party, which sees the zombies kill everyone apart from one girl who manages to escape. She reminds Colin of his girlfriend Laura and he goes after her, but she is captured by a crazed man who keeps zombies in his basement.

Linda isn't about to give up on her brother, and with the help of a friend manages to take him to their mum's house. But he has bitten her earlier and she now turns into a zombie. The two of them leave and go on the hunt for more humans to kill. They join a big group of zombies but come under attack when a few surviving humans decide to fight back and Colin ends up having part of his face blown off by a grenade.

He goes to his girlfriend Laura's home and a flashback shows him in the same house. He is human and Laura comes under attack by a zombie, but she manages to trap it in the bathroom. However, it bites

her when she tries to kill it and she dies. Colin holds
her lifeless body but she reanimates into a zombie. She
bites him and he is forced to kill her before escaping to
Damien's house. This is how he got the injuries that
turned him into a zombie at the start of the movie.

Colin started out being played at various film festivals
around the world, including Cannes, before receiving a
limited cinema release and coming out on DVD. It was
a big hit with zombie movie critics. Horror magazine
SCARS said it would 'revolutionize zombie cinema'
and the website Zombie Friends thought it was 'as
original, compelling and thought provoking as [George
A] Romero's *Night of the Living Dead*'. DJ Benz from
the website Horror Talk ended his review by saying:
'*Colin* is one of those rare gems of independent cinema,
one that brings new ideas, talent and faces to the screen.
I've no doubt it will be a huge hit with horror fans and
I can only hope that some enterprising distributor picks
it up and gives it the release it deserves.'

Journalist Peter Bradshaw might have given the film
only three out of five stars in the *Guardian* but he still
applauded the director and cast for what they had
managed to produce on their tiny budget. '*Colin* is an
ultra-minimal, ultra-experimental future-shock in the
tradition of *The War Game*, *Survivors* and *Threads*,' he
wrote. 'A nuclear war in the US has caused a viral
catastrophe here. Corpses have come back to life, biting
the healthy and spreading the disease. One such is

Colin, whose sister refuses to kill him. Price focuses as much on human drama and social breakdown as on the zombie phenomenon. As for the undead gamely played by Price's mates, the acting and gurning and ketchup are a little broad, sure. But if there ever was a zombie calamity on Britain's streets, I have a sinking feeling that it would look exactly like the cheap absurdist nightmare shown here.'

DID YOU KNOW?

The big battle scene was shot in London without a filming permit. Marc Price could have been in serious trouble but thankfully the policeman sent to investigate the 'riot' wasn't too bothered and just took a few photos of his own. He had arrived to scenes of mass carnage with bits of bodies and fake blood everywhere but was quickly brought up to speed on what was going on. The director was prepared for the policeman being a stickler for the rules. As he went over to talk to him with an empty camera, the actual tape was being hidden by another crew member.

D IS FOR...

DAWN OF THE DEAD (1978)

Written and directed by George A Romero, *Dawn of the Dead* was the second movie in his Dead series. George and his team shot the movie over four months in Pittsburgh and nearby Monroeville, Pennsylvania. The shopping mall used in the movie was the Monroeville mall. On its release, *Dawn of the Dead* was a box office hit and earned around $55 million from screenings around the world. Despite its violent nature and gruesome storyline, it gained rave reviews from critics and has been loved by horror fans ever since. In

2008 the movie featured in *Empire* magazine's 'Top 500 Greatest Movies of All Time'.

The movie starts with an outbreak of an unknown disease that has swept across America, killing civilians and bringing them back to life as flesh-eating zombies. The government and authorities across the country attempt to control the outbreak and the terror, but without much success in the cities and towns. However, rural parts of the country are more successful in controlling the undead because of the lower number of people in these areas.

People in the cities are panicking and will do anything to make sure they are safe, with little regard for anyone else. Stephen (David Emge) is a pilot for the traffic news at Philadelphia television station WGON, and he and his girlfriend Francine (Gaylen Ross) plot to steal the company helicopter in a bid to escape the zombie attackers.

On the other side of town, Roger (Scott Reiniger) and his SWAT team raid an apartment block where residents are refusing to give over their diseased loved ones to the National Guard. Gunfire breaks out between the residents and the SWAT team. The residents are killed, some by the SWAT team and some by their relatives and neighbours who have become undead. During the raid, Roger meets Peter (Ken Foree) from another SWAT team and together they kill all the remaining zombies they find shut in the basement of the apartment building by the former residents.

Roger tells Peter of his, Stephen and Francine's plan to escape and together the four of them fly off in search of refuge, battling the zombies they come across on their way. The four touch down and hole up in a shopping mall. They barricade the door with big trucks to stop more zombies getting in but Roger is bitten by one of them. As he starts to deteriorate he asks Peter to shoot him so he doesn't come back and try to attack the group. Also, during their time in the mall Francine discovers she is pregnant.

The friends are interrupted when some bikers break into the mall seeking refuge but end up having a shoot-out with Stephen. To make matters worse, the bikers let zombies into the mall. These manage to find Stephen, who has been shot, and eat him in the elevator. Most of the bikers get slaughtered by the zombies; the rest retreat.

To add to the drama, Stephen becomes reanimated and leads a group of zombies to where his girlfriend, unborn child and Peter are hiding. Peter kills Stephen and the zombies accompanying him and then escapes with Francine to the roof of the mall, where they take off in the helicopter but with little fuel in the tank…

DID YOU KNOW?

The director had a different ending planned for the movie, where Peter commits suicide by shooting himself in the head and Francine kills herself by putting her head in the blades of the helicopter. The credits would roll and the scene would show the helicopter's engine slowing down, symbolising that, with little fuel, the pair would have died anyway.

MOVIE MISTAKES

When Roger is driving the truck and hits the zombie, you can see the stunt man's trampoline at the bottom right-hand side.

When Roger parked the first truck and ran over to Peter in the other truck, he passed a zombie wearing a red and black rugby shirt. The zombie stops what he is doing and checks that his shirt is tucked in.

When Peter and Roger are using the trucks to block the entrances, Roger kills a zombie with a long beard but in a later scene the same zombie is shown trying to get into the shopping mall.

DAWN OF THE DEAD (2004)

Released by Universal Studios in 2004, this remake was directed by Zack Snyder and produced by Strike Entertainment in association with New Amsterdam Entertainment.

The movie starts with a nurse called Ana (Sarah Polley), who has worked a long shift at the hospital, returning home to her husband Luis in their home town in Wisconsin. The couple miss an urgent news broadcast on the TV warning of zombie attacks happening across the country, and the next day a zombie child breaks into their house and kills Luis. Instantly he comes back to life as a zombie and attacks his wife, who only just manages to escape in her car. She is in such a panic that she crashes it and passes out.

The zombies are taking over the country. When Ana comes to she is joined by police sergeant Kenneth Hall (Ving Rhames), jack of all trades Michael (Jake Weber), petty criminal Andre (Mekhi Phifer) and his pregnant wife Luda. The group seek refuge in a nearby shopping mall but a zombie security guard attacks Luda, biting her. The other security guards – Terry, Bart and CJ – are still human and join the group.

Together they barricade the mall to stop more killer zombies entering and then head for the roof of the building. They see a man called Andy at the other side of the car park but he is trapped in a gun store and they have no way of getting to him because there are so many zombies by the store.

The next day a truck arrives with more survivors: Tucker, Monica, Norma, Glen, Steve, Frank and his daughter Nicole. An ill woman is with them too, but she dies and comes back as a zombie, so she is killed by the group. The gang realises the disease is spread by being bitten by a zombie, so Frank – who has been bitten – decides to isolate himself from the group and is shot later on. A worried Andre sees to his pregnant wife, who has also been bitten. He knows she will reanimate and become a danger to everyone around her.

One night the group has dinner together and is bonding over food when the power cuts out. CJ, Bart, Michael and Kenneth go to switch on the emergency generator up in the car park. Zombies attack them and kill Bart. The rest get stuck in the generator room with the zombies, which they kill by pouring gas over them and setting them alight.

During all this Luda has been tied up by Andre but becomes more ill and dies while giving birth. Luda comes back as a zombie but is then shot by Norma. Andre goes mad and shoots at Norma and they both die in the gunfight. Only the zombie baby is left alive but it is soon killed when the others return.

The remaining survivors plot to escape on Steve's yacht to an island on Lake Michigan because they know they can't stay in the shopping mall for much longer. The group plans to get to the marina by reinforcing two shuttle buses and escaping in them.

Andy, who is still stuck in the gun shop across the car park, is dying of starvation and they want to help him. They send a dog, which they found earlier, across the car park with food strapped to its back. But when Andy opens the door, the undead get in and he reincarnates as a zombie. Overly sensitive Nicole stupidly drives a truck into the gun shop to check if the dog is OK, only to be trapped by zombie Andy. Tucker, Terry, CJ, Kenneth and Michael come to her rescue through the sewers that run underneath the car park. They kill Andy, save Nicole, and try to take as many weapons as they can from the gun store. Tucker gets killed but everyone else is OK and they all get onto the buses.

During their escape, Glen foolishly loses control of the chainsaw he is holding and not only kills himself but Monica too. Blood sprays everywhere, covering the windscreen of the bus and causing them to crash. Steve gets killed by a zombie and Ana kills him as soon as he comes back as one. Ana then takes the keys for the yacht from Steve's corpse and the remaining survivors flee to the marina. CJ gives himself up to the zombies so the rest can escape, and Michael kills himself after a zombie bites him.

The five remaining members of the group escape on the yacht but run out of food. When they arrive on the nearest island, more zombies appear and the movie ends with a camcorder found on Steve's boat recording them being chased by the flesh-eating zombies. There was no escape!

MOVIE MISTAKES

When pregnant Luda washes blood off her top you can see her stomach is flat when it should have a big bump.

After giving birth, Luda is shot through the left eye and her socket is obliterated, but when the others return and survey the scene she still has her left eye.

When Tucker and Steve look through binoculars to see Andy kill a zombie, their binoculars still have their lens caps on.

DAY OF THE DEAD (1985)

Day of the Dead was the third movie in George A Romero's Dead series. Reviewers and fans deemed it the weakest of the three movies but it still managed to achieve a respectable score of 79 out of 100 on Rotten Tomatoes.

The movie is set after *Dawn of the Dead* and starts with Dr Sarah Bowman (Lori Cardille) and her crew being sent out in search of survivors. They fly over the coast of Florida and land in Fort Myers, a small suburban city. The crew walk the streets calling out in search of survivors, only to bring a swarm of undead towards them. The crew – including pilot John (Terry Alexander) and his Irish pal Bill (Jarlath Conroy) – quickly retreat to their base in an underground army bunker out in the swamps.

Sarah's crew consists of a group of military-supported scientists under orders to find a cure and stop the attack of the undead on the nation. Orders from what little of the US government is left imply that they need to find a way to reverse the spread or stop it. The crew's leader, Major Cooper, died on their expedition, so Captain Rhodes (Joseph Pilato) is put in charge of the operation.

Rhodes sets up a meeting to try to raise the group's morale, but arguments break out over conflicting ideas of what research they should be focusing on. Private Miguel Salazar (Anthony Dileo Jr) is a highly stressed soldier who is heading for a mental breakdown. To make matters worse, Private Steel attacks him in anger after his lack of focus nearly causes Private Rickles to die. Scientist Logan believes that Sarah's research is too focused on reversing the zombification of humans, whereas his research is about their behaviour and being able to control what they do.

Logan, the head scientist on the operation, has been sneakily using dead soldiers to experiment on, the most recent being his former leader Major Cooper. An argument begins between Sarah and Logan, as Sarah is worried that Rhodes will kill them both if he finds out what Logan is doing. Logan explains his theory that zombies can be trained. He believes they work on primeval instincts alone, not the vitamins and nutrients needed by human flesh. His convincing talk gains him permission to continue his research. The next day Logan demonstrates his new zombie specimen, Bub. The docile specimen has little memory of the past but is able to identify household items, which in Rhodes' opinion is a waste of valuable scientific time.

When testing on a different zombie, another one breaks free, attacking Private Miller by ripping his throat out. During the scuffle Miller kills Private Johnson with the gun he was holding. Private Steel then tries to kill the zombified Miller, while Miguel attempts to kill the escaped zombie, only to be bitten. Sarah comes to Miguel's rescue by quickly amputating his arm and sealing the wound to stop Miguel from turning into a zombie. With Bill's help she stops the rest of the soldiers from killing Miguel. The soldiers retreat, and Bill and Sarah try to find painkillers for Miguel.

While searching for the medication, they come across a tape recorder and the decapitated head of the recently deceased Private Johnson. There are wires fused to the head and it is making noises. The tape recorder has a recording of Logan talking to his mother and himself. Listening to the recording makes Bill and Sarah wonder if Logan is insane, as he chants: 'Its mind's talking – it's talking!'

Sarah, Bill, John and Miguel question whether they should escape in their helicopter but Rhodes finds the remains of his dead soldiers in Logan's freezer and kills Logan. He takes Sarah, Bill and Fisher (another scientist), removes their guns, and orders John to fly him and his men out of the swamp. John refuses. Rhodes shoots Fisher to make his point and shoves Sarah and Bill into the cage for zombie specimens. John knocks out Rhodes and makes a run for it with Sarah and Bill.

Back in the underground bunker the lift starts to make a noise and Privates Steel and Rickles go to see why. When they get to the lift, they find that Miguel has escaped in it and has torn the controls out, so the rest are now stuck underground. Miguel then sacrifices himself and lets the zombies down into the bunker. Rhodes escapes, leaving his men in the bunker. Two die, ripped apart by zombies, but Steel makes it out, only to be confronted with a line of zombies. He shoots himself in the mouth before they kill him.

Meanwhile zombie specimen Bud has got hold of some of the soldiers' weapons and, angry about the murder of his master Dr Logan, shoots Rhodes, who is then decapitated by other zombies. As he dies he shouts: 'CHOKE ON 'EM!'

The three survivors – Sarah, John and Bill – race for the helicopter, which may or may not have any fuel left, but they suffer attacks from zombies on their way. John and Bill shoot while Sarah opens the helicopter's door, only to find more arms clutching at her...

The film closes with Sarah waking up from a nightmare as she lies on a tropical beach, while John and Bill are off fishing.

DID YOU KNOW?

George wanted this to be the finale to his series and to be the best movie of the three. However, due to financial cuts, the film's budget was axed by around half, causing the script to be altered to fit a smaller budget.

The directors of some modern-day zombie movies show their respect for George's work by including aspects or lines from his movies in their films. In *28 Days Later*, the British soldiers are in charge of holding 'infected' humans for testing purposes. In *Resident Evil* there is a shot of Alice walking the streets past a newspaper blowing in the wind with 'The Dead Walk' written on its pages.

MOVIE MISTAKES

In the abandoned city, at first the alligator on the bank's steps doesn't have anything covering its mouth, but when the zombie runs down the steps the beast has a red band on its mouth to stop it biting the actor.

When Sarah is cutting off Miguel's arm with the machete, the camera moves closer and we can see fake blood coming from her hand.

When Steel and Miguel are out getting more zombie specimens, Steel says, 'Nice hat, asshole!' and laughs, but the laugh was added later and his mouth doesn't move.

DEAD SET (2008)

Dead Set was a Channel 4/E4 zombie mini-series created by journalist and comic writer Charlie Brooker. A big hit with critics and viewers, it was nominated for a BAFTA in the Best Drama Serial category but sadly lost out to BBC1's *Criminal Justice*.

Dead Set tells the story of a zombie outbreak that affects the whole of the UK but leaves the contestants in the *Big Brother* house clueless as to what has happened until they too come under attack. (Brooker got the idea while watching *24*.) It was shown for the first time in the run-up to Halloween and the first episode was watched by 1.5 million people. Indeed, it proved so popular that Channel 4 bosses decided to show it again during one of the *Celebrity Big Brother* weeks the following year.

Donkey Punch actress Jaime Winstone played Kelly, the show's runner. Magician and actor Andy Nyman played the show's sleazy producer Patrick, comedian Kevin Eldon played the housemate Joplin, *Four Lions* actor Riz Ahmed played Riq, *The Bill* actress Beth Cordingly played Veronica and *Wedding Belles* actress Kathleen McDermott played Pippa. Davina McCall and several contestants from past *Big Brother* series played themselves. Davina said she enjoyed turning into a zombie and based her zombie run on the assassin T-1000 from the movie *Terminator 2: Judgment Day*.

The series was directed by Yann Demange, best known for directing the Channel 4 comedy drama *A Man in a Box* and Billie Piper's *Secret Diary of a Call Girl*. One of the biggest challenges Yann faced when directing *Dead Set* was the budget, as there were times when he couldn't do exactly what he and Charlie Brooker wanted. He had to have some of the zombie extras double up because the special contact lenses they needed were expensive, and a car-crash scene had to be changed to a 'car breaks down' scene as they didn't have enough money for explosions. As in the movie *Colin*, Facebook was used to recruit zombies.

Charlie Brooker is a huge fan of zombie movies, so

he loved having the opportunity to make his own, albeit a mini-series. He explained to E4 why he loves zombies: 'What I like about zombies is that they are thick. I don't like watching horror films about, say, a serial killer, where the villain is a brilliant intellectual, and could also double as the controller of Radio 3. The serial killer is always one step ahead of the police, and taunting them. Whereas most serial killers, in reality, are so mentally deranged that they wouldn't be like that. And I don't really relate to vampires or ghosts. I don't find them particularly frightening.

'In the original Romero movies, zombies were this big dumb mass of stupidity. The protagonists always get complacent, because these things are shambling around quite slowly and can't keep up with them. And then by sheer weight of numbers they get overwhelmed. So if you live in a city, you're surrounded by people constantly. If you imagine something suddenly afflicted them all, and they were all coming after you, then you're in big trouble. It's a fear of an anonymous mass coming after you. Except, of course, modern-day zombies have evolved. They learned to run in about 2002. Which is probably good: it gives the genre a new lease of life.'

Charlie particularly wanted to play a zombie in *Dead Set* but it wasn't as big a role as he would have liked. 'I have a little cameo,' he explained. 'What was frustrating was that I couldn't be a featured zombie – I had to be a B–list zombie. I was supposed to be a featured zombie, but my eyes are too weird and bug-like. They couldn't put the contact lenses on me. They tried shoving them in for about 15 minutes, and every time I blinked they came out. My eyelids are too thin or something.'

In the first episode, it is a *Big Brother* eviction night like no other. There are mass riots all around the country but the *Big Brother* contestants have no idea of what is happening. Davina is getting ready to evict the housemate with the smallest number of votes but she is concerned that the show might be ditched for the news, because of the riots everywhere. Some former housemates are gathered in the green room for a special edition of *Big Brother's Little Brother*. Runner Kelly and assistant Claire are doing the bidding of a very stressed producer, Patrick. Elsewhere, Riq, Kelly's boyfriend, is wondering what to do after his car is stolen and he is stuck at a train station.

Inside the house, Pippa, Veronica, Grayson, Marky, Space, Angel and Joplin are waiting to see who will be the next housemate to be evicted. Pippa's mum is on her way to the studio with her injured driver and a runner but when they arrive the driver dies from his injuries and reanimates. Pippa's mum, the runner and a security guard don't stand a chance and are quickly killed by him. The security guard reanimates and starts killing members of the *Big Brother* audience. They too reanimate and before long there are zombies everywhere. They manage to break into the building and turn several members of the production crew, the former housemates and Davina into zombies.

Kelly and Patrick manage to survive, but only just. Patrick ends up giving Claire and a disabled man to the zombies so he can escape and he hides in a toilet; Kelly manages to survive after hiding in an office. As Patrick tries to escape a zombie Davina, he finds Pippa, the evicted housemate. The housemates still inside the *Big Brother* house have no idea what is going on and when Kelly appears they think she is a new housemate and don't believe what she tells them. They think it's just a massive hoax and Marky opens one of the doors, which lets in a zombie. Angel is bitten, but, before anyone else can be attacked, Kelly kills it with a fire extinguisher to the head.

In the second episode Riq has moved from the train station to a petrol station but things are looking bleak until he is rescued by Alex, another survivor. They think they will be safe if they get to the coast, but when the car they are travelling in breaks down, they become sitting ducks. Alex shoots the zombies that come across them while Riq tries to fix the car, but tensions run high and they argue. When they hear a large group of zombies heading their way, they decide to get out while they can and run. They find an empty house to hide in.

Meanwhile, back in the *Big Brother* compound,

Patrick and Pippa are still trapped as Davina is outside the green room. The housemates and Kelly are wondering what to do next as Angel might reanimate. Grayson is a nurse and thinks he could help her if he had the right equipment and supplies. They put Angel in the greenhouse so they can keep a close eye on her and Grayson is instructed to stab Angel in the head straight away if she does turn into a zombie.

The rest of the housemates decide that they need to get food if they are to survive. Joplin and Veronica climb on the roof and bang pots to try to distract the zombies while the others make a break for it. Kelly and Space make it to a van but Marky is chased by a zombie and only just manages to jump in the back in time. Others quickly follow.

In the third episode, the three of them make it to the supermarket but Marky picks up an injury to his arm from the tools in the back of the van. Two policemen are there too, looking for looters. One gets bitten so his friend kills him quickly before he can reanimate. The other policeman thinks Marky's injury is a bite and wants to kill him, but before he can, Kelly shoots him in the leg. They leave him behind when more zombies arrive.

Back in the *Big Brother* house things are getting messy as Angel becomes a zombie. Grayson is bitten and Angel then turns her attention on Veronica. Before she can kill her, Grayson throws Angel into the pool before the others kill him. They stab him in the head just moments before Kelly, Space and Marky return. Kelly shoots Angel, who can't seem to get out of the pool. The zombies might be relatively dumb but they are still a huge threat because there are so many of them.

Riq and Alex decide to leave the house and make their way to the *Big Brother* studio after Riq sees the live feed on E4 when he turns on the TV. They don't have many options left as they find out from the radio that a rescue boat has left for France with the only other survivors. They have been left behind.

In the fourth episode, Riq decides he wants to be with Kelly and convinces Alex that they will be able to make it to the *Big Brother* studios if they go by boat down the river. They set out but a zombie attacks Alex as she tries to open the lock gate and Riq is forced to kill her with her own axe so she doesn't reanimate.

Patrick and Pippa finally manage to leave the green room and make it to the main house after killing Davina. Patrick tries to convince everyone that it is best to leave while they can and try to make it to the coast, but the others aren't convinced. They have seen how many zombies are at the gates and know they wouldn't stand a chance.

Patrick doesn't care what they think and starts chopping up Grayson's body and placing bits of him in a bowl so he can use them to distract the zombies. Marky and Kelly head for the roof and Marky starts shooting any zombies that come within range. Riq arrives but Marky thinks he's a zombie so he starts shooting at him.

In the fifth episode, Riq manages to take cover and he narrowly misses being shot by Marky. Kelly recognises his voice and tells Marky to stop before letting Riq in through the gates. She kisses him and thinks he's come to rescue her, but he explains that the zombies are everywhere and they are safer where they are. Patrick still thinks they should take their bowl of flesh and try to escape the way Riq came in, but the others tie him up. Patrick manages to convince Joplin to go against the others and gets Joplin to untie him. The two men take Kelly as their hostage and head outside. The others follow to try to get Kelly back, but Riq ends up getting killed by Patrick. Pippa can't take any more and runs off, with Space trying to catch up with her. Joplin has totally lost the plot and opens the gates, letting the huge group of zombies in.

Joplin is quickly killed and the others run inside. Patrick tries to use his bowl of flesh to satisfy the zombies who come close, but it isn't enough and he soon dies, complaining as they rip him apart. Space makes it to the control booth but is bitten. Kelly gets inside the diary room but Veronica and Marky aren't so lucky. Both Space and Kelly are trapped. Zombies are pounding on the glass trying to get into the control booth and Space recognises one of them as Pippa. Kelly tells him he's the winner of this series of *Big Brother* and asks him to open the door so she can leave the diary room. He doesn't want to but she insists, as she thinks she can make it. On her command, he does as she asks, and she screams as the camera cuts to black. He's the only one left...

As the cameras scan the *Big Brother* compound, the former housemates are shown as zombies, eating the corpses and walking around. As zombie Kelly looks at the camera, the live feed is shown on TV sets in an electrical store and a zombie watches what is going on.

Both lovers and haters of *Big Brother* enjoyed *Dead Set* and it became a popular talking point in workplaces, schools and colleges up and down the country. People loved the idea of seeing Brian Belo (Series 8, winner), Imogen Thomas (Series 7, seventh place), Helen Adams (Series 2, second place), Aisleyne Horgan-Wallace (Series 7, third place), Paul Ferguson/Bubble (Series 1, eighth place), Saskia Howard-Clarke (Series 6, eleventh place), Eugene Sully (Series 7, second place), Ziggy Lichman (Series 8, fourth place), Makosi Musambasi (Series 6, third place) and Kinga Karolczak (Series 6, fourth place) turn into zombies!

Critics enjoyed it too. Martin Anderson from the website Den of Geek wrote in his review: 'If *Dead Set* is not original (*Wrong Turn 2* having stolen the march on injecting reality TV into genre horror), it is nonetheless gripping, and a quantum leap in quality for E4. Brooker has gnawed off the best parts of countless zombie movies and strewn them through his script, sometimes digested (the "wheelchair zombie" is a nice wrinkle) and sometimes not: the reference to *The Living Dead at the Manchester Morgue* is nicely elliptical, although Marky's aping of a scene from *Night of the Living Dead* rather dents Brooker's portrayal of a world that seems to have no zombies in its entertainment culture.

'Ultimately *Dead Set* is likely to engage even *Big Brother*-haters in the very rubber-necking they protest in the show itself, but now with a protective cushion of fiction. Prickly, world-hating Patrick is obviously being set up for a 'Rhodes special' from the original *Day of the Dead*, but – like the original – it mustn't happen until the end; he's the only one who can really see the guts of the situation, his acidic cynicism impervious even to zombie onslaught.'

Simon Pegg was complimentary about the series in his review for the *Guardian* but there was one aspect he didn't like. 'The concept was clever in its simplicity,' he wrote. 'A full-scale zombie outbreak coincides with a *Big Brother* eviction night, leaving the *Big Brother* house as the last refuge for the survivors. Scripted by Charlie Brooker, a writer whose scalpel-sharp incisiveness I have long been a fan of, and featuring talented actors such as Jaime Winstone and the outstanding Kevin Eldon, the show heralded the arrival of genuine home-grown horror, scratching at the fringes of network television. My expectations were high, and I sat down to watch a show that proved smart, inventive and enjoyable, but for one key detail: ZOMBIES DON'T RUN!

'I know it is absurd to debate the rules of a reality that does not exist, but this genuinely irks me. You cannot kill a vampire with an MDF stake; were-wolves can't fly; zombies do not run. It's a misconception, a bastardisation that diminishes a classic movie monster. The best phantasmagoria uses reality to render the inconceivable conceivable. The speedy zombie seems implausible to me, even within the fantastic realm it inhabits. A biological agent, I'll buy. Some sort of super-virus? Sure, why not. But death? Death is a disability, not a superpower. It's hard to run with a cold, let alone the most debilitating malady of them all.'

Charlie Brooker responded in his article in the *Guardian* the following week, giving five reasons why the zombies in *Dead Set* could run: '1) I like running zombies. I just do. 2) They HAD to run or the story wouldn't work. The outbreak had to knock the entire country out of action before the producers had time to evacuate the studios. 3) We had to clearly and immediately differentiate *Dead Set* from *Shaun of the Dead*, which had cornered the market on zombie-centric horror-comedy. Blame yourself, Simon: if you'd made that film badly, it wouldn't have been so popular, and drawing a distinction wouldn't have been an issue. Each time one of our zombies breaks into a sprint, it's your own stupid talented fault.

'4) Even George Romero, the godfather of zombies, bent the rules from time to time. Witness the very first zombie in *Night of the Living Dead*, which moves at a fair old whack and even picks up a rock to try to smash a car window. Or the two kiddywink zombies in *Dawn of the Dead*, who burst out of a room and run – yes, run – towards Ken Foree. I know you saw these scenes. You know you saw these scenes. And you also know that if this were a trial, this would be the moment where you splutter in the witness box and admit you're completely wrong.

'5) Running zombies are, to be frank, cheaper than stumbling ones. You only need one or two to present a massive threat. I love a huge mass of shambling undead as much as the next guy, but we couldn't afford that many crowd scenes. The original plan was to set the final episode six months in the future, by which time the zombies were badly decayed and could only shuffle (although "freshies" would still run), but budget and time constraints ruled this out. Which would you rather see – running zombies or absolutely no zombies at all? Hmm? HMM?

'Face facts. It's time to embrace diversity, Simon.

Make room in your heart for all breeds of zombie. Except ones that talk. They're just silly.'

TOP THREE QUOTES

Space: 'Something is wrong… No mics, no alarms and the cameras ain't movin'. *Big Brother* ain't watchin' us!'

Veronica: 'Does it mean we're not on telly anymore?'

Pippa: 'Is that Davina?'
Patrick: 'Sort of.'

DID YOU KNOW?

In the script Charlie Brooker pays tribute to some iconic zombie films. When Kelly explains that zombies have taken over, he has Marky call Grayson 'Barbra' (the name of one of the characters from *Night of the Living Dead*) and quote the first line from the film ('They're coming to get you, Barbra!'). In another scene Charlie has Joplin paraphrase one of the lines from *Dawn of the Dead* when he says: 'Some primitive instinct… this was like a church for them!'

DEATHDREAM/DEAD OF NIGHT (1974)

Deathdream is an iconic zombie movie which was released on 30 August 1974. It was directed by Bob Clark, who is most famous for directing and co-writing the 1983 movie *A Christmas Story*. The writer Alan Ormsby provided the script for *Deathdream*. As well as being a screenwriter he is also an author, director and actor.

Deathdream was inspired by the short story 'The Monkey's Paw' by WW Jacobs. It starred Richard Backus as Andy Brooks, Lynn Carlin as Christine Brooks and John Marley as Charles Brooks. Its working title was 'The Veteran'.

The movie starts with two US soldiers walking through some trees and getting shot. The second soldier to be targeted by the sniper is Andy Brooks, and, as the bullet hits him, he hears his mother's voice telling him: 'Andy, you'll come back, you've got to, you promised.'

Andy's family is later informed that he has passed away. His father Charles and sister Cathy accept that he has gone but his mother Christine can't believe that he is dead and is adamant that he is still alive. The family goes to bed but in the middle of the night they find Andy has returned. They can't believe it at first but are so happy that Andy didn't die after all.

Andy is different, and as the days pass they notice his strange behaviour. He prefers to spend his days alone in a dark room sitting on a rocking chair and he wears dark glasses, gloves and clothes that cover up his body. At night he goes out and kills people, using a syringe to take their blood and transferring it to himself to stop the decomposition process. His mother fails to recognise that something isn't right.

A double date with his girlfriend and best friend turns into a bloodbath as Andy attacks the girls and ends up killing his friend. As Andy tries to make his escape in the car he is chased by the police. He takes them to the local cemetery and they find Andy's remains in a shallow grave. He has scratched Andy Brooks 1951–1971 on the tombstone. Christine appears and tells the policemen: 'Andy's home; some boys never come home.'

DIARY OF THE DEAD (2007)

Independently produced, this gruesome horror movie was the fifth in George A Romero's Dead series. In it, a group of film students are caught up in an outbreak of zombies. They decide to make their own documentary about it but risk being killed. The movie is a re-imagining rather than a follow-on from the previous movies in the series and the story starts on day one of the outbreak.

When George was asked by Capone from the

website Ain't It Cool News why he had decided to start from the beginning again, he replied: 'You know, it's complicated to answer that because I don't know how to shorthand this... After *Land of the Dead*, I thought things had gotten very big; it was going *Thunderdome*.

'I said, where do I go from here? *Beyond the Planet of the Apes*? I just wanted to go back to do something small, and I had the idea that I wanted to do something about this emerging media culture that we're in. And I thought, well, perfect way. So I thought, I'll go back to the first night... There's a series of short stories called *Book of the Dead*. Major science-fiction and horror writers contributed stories to this, including Steve King. And I said, I can do that too. I'll just go back to the first night. I wanted to use film students who were out shooting their own class project.

'They have a camera, and the shit hits the fan, and they start to document it. But if it's three years into the phenomenon, they wouldn't be going to class any more. So, it all just fell into place. I wanted to drop back; I wanted to do something smaller. I wanted to get back to the roots a little bit, and I had this idea. It's all timing, and timing is everything, and it came together.'

The opening scene in the movie is a news report of a family who have all died in their apartment. As the family are wheeled out by the paramedics on medical trolleys, the mother and daughter wake up, looking like they are in some sort of trance, and leap at the paramedics, attacking them. The two also manage to bite some of the crowd who are watching before being shot.

While the news is being reported, film studies students at the University of Pittsburgh are working on a project they have been given to make their own horror film. The students are out filming in nearby woods with their professor, Andrew Maxwell. They give their film the title *The Dead of Death*. After they introduce their film, the camera cuts to the students acting out the scene of a mummy in the woods. Professor Maxwell is advising Ridley, who is playing the character of the mummy, about how he should capture the movements of a corpse. The group begin to argue with the make-up artist, Tony (Shawn Roberts), for not doing a good enough job on the actor who is playing the zombie.

While the group are bickering, fellow student Eliot (Joe Dinicol) brings their attention to the events being recorded on the news. The radio warns of a severe wave of violence and murder spreading across the nation: the dead are walking, killing people and eating them. After hearing the reports the group split up. Ridley decides to take his girlfriend Francine home to Philadelphia because he thinks they will be safe there. The director of the film, Jason (Joshua

Close), is excited because they can use what is happening in their horror film.

Jason leaves the woods and heads to the dorm of his girlfriend Debra (Michelle Morgan) but she is distressed because she can't get hold of her family and she wants to know that they are safe. Jason, Debra and their friends decide to drive to Scranton, Pennsylvania, to check on Debra's family. Jason films them as Mary drives the RV and he gets everyone to introduce themselves. Their film is now going to be a documentary of what is happening.

On the drive down the group witness a car accident at the side of the road. A highway patrolman stumbles towards them but in fear Mary drives away, hitting three zombies as she tries to escape from them. When the car stops, Mary shoots herself in the head with a gun. The rest of the group rush her to hospital, but when they get there Mary reanimates. The professor shoots her before she can cause any harm but Gordo gets bitten by another zombie and dies. Tracy begs her friends not to shoot him when he reanimates but he goes to attack her and she's forced to kill him. All this is recorded for the documentary.

The group realise that they will have to kill the zombies who cross their path if they are going to make it to Scranton. They get back in their RV but after a while they break down when the fuel line snaps. They are helped by Samuel, a deaf Amish man who lives nearby. The group seek refuge from the attacks of the undead in a barn, but it is soon surrounded by zombies. During the ambush Samuel fights them off and Tracy manages to repair the RV. The group leave quickly but have to leave Samuel behind as he has been bitten and will reanimate soon.

As they continue their journey, the group pass through a city that has been destroyed by the zombies. They come across a group of survivors, led by a National Guardsman with whom they negotiate to get extra weapons and ammunition. The Guardsman tells the group that he has little faith in the military controlling or helping in the situation as they seem to have been abandoned by everyone.

Jason and Debra start to argue because Debra has discovered that her family were away camping and are only just heading home now, so there was no need for her panic and for the group to travel all this way. She is annoyed at how much Jason is filming because he seems to care more about the film than their safety. Jason disagrees and says the film will be his way of showing the rest of the world what has happened.

The group led by the National Guard have a scare when one of the soldiers who has died of a heart attack goes missing, and one of the group accidentally ends up killing one of their own men in the hunt for the zombie soldier. Eventually they track the zombie down to a petrol station and kill him using a hydrochloric acid canister.

Jason takes time out to upload his recent footage to the internet and almost immediately he receives 72,000 responses from people around the world. The student group decide it is time to leave, gathering supplies and heading to Debra's parents' house, after she receives a text from her little brother saying the family have arrived home safely. Before they leave, Jason receives a video call from classmate Ridley, who has headed back to his mansion home in Philadelphia. Ridley tells the group that he and his girlfriend Francine are safe and invites them over to seek refuge with them. As they leave, Tony shows his survival instincts by killing a zombie that appears and tries to attack them.

Upon arrival they discover Debra's family's car with a shattered passenger window and blood everywhere. The group search the house and discover the body of Debra's little brother, who suddenly awakens and tries to attack Debra, but is killed by the professor just in time. The group then find Debra's mother zombified and feasting on her husband. The professor kills her and then they all leave for Ridley's mansion home.

On their journey to Philadelphia the group come across a group of soldiers who demand that they stop filming. Suddenly they strip the students and their professor of all weapons and supplies and drive off, leaving the group worried as they have no supplies or way to defend themselves against zombie attackers, only their vehicle.

After a few hours' driving, the group arrive at the mansion, only to find the front door wide open and the place apparently deserted. The group start searching the house and come across an old bookcase that doubles as a panic room, which holds a rather frightened-looking Ridley. The panic room has a two-foot-wide steel door and is equipped with video cameras and monitors showing the entire grounds of the mansion. He tells his classmates that his father, mother and servants all turned into zombies and Francine was attacked by the family's butler.

Jason and Tracy head back to the car to unload their belongings. Tony takes charge of the camera, filming Ridley rummaging for food in his kitchen. Listening to his story, Debra and Tony go with Ridley to where he says he buried his family and household staff. As they walk, Tony notices a bite mark on Ridley's hand. When they get to the pool house Ridley locks them inside and Debra and Tony see that he lied and that he dumped the bodies in the swimming pool instead.

Ridley turns and heads to where Tracy and Jason are unloading the car. As he does so, he starts to transform into a zombie. He tries to attack Tracy, who runs away from him. Ridley is then distracted by Jason, who is filming the action, and Tracy knocks him out. In the meantime the professor has locked himself in the panic room with a shotgun after seeing things unfold. Tracy leaves in the RV, angry that she had to stop Ridley because Jason was too busy filming to help her.

The following morning (with the camera still rolling), the remaining survivors are awakened by the former servants, now zombies, breaking into the mansion. After witnessing Ridley waking up and murdering Eliot by pushing him into a bathtub to electrocute him, the professor insists that the group retreat to the panic room. Jason protests, saying he does not want to be shut off from the outside world, and as the rest of the group stock up on supplies in the panic room, he secretly disappears in search of some footage of zombie Ridley.

Jason finds Ridley and inevitably is attacked and bitten by him. In the nick of time, the professor finds the pair and stabs Ridley in the head with a sword he has found. Jason is then shot by Debra, after the professor warns her that he will come back as a zombie if she doesn't do it straight away. After she has killed him, Debra picks up his camcorder and watches his last moments. She tells the others that, in his memory, she will continue filming what he had started.

The remaining three – Debra, the professor and Tony – lock themselves in the panic room after seeing hundreds of zombies swarming the mansion, one of which is their former classmate Eliot. Debra sits down in the panic room and continues to watch Jason's footage. With the realisation that they have no escape route out of the panic room and the knowledge that there are hundreds of zombies on the other side of the steel door wanting to eat them, life seems to be over for the trio.

The movie ends with Debra watching Jason's latest download, of a group of men tying dead bodies to a tree and using them as target practice. She considers whether the fight for survival and to save the human race is so necessary when humans do such inhumane things.

Jamie Russell of the BBC wrote in his review of the movie: 'The zombies may be dead but George Romero's taste for social commentary certainly isn't in *Diary of the Dead*, the latest instalment in his long-running walking corpse series. Forty years after the Pittsburgh filmmaker unleashed the modern zombie movie in *Night of the Living Dead*, he returns to dissect our media-saturated culture as it heads down the YouTube. Josh Close stars as Jason, a student filmmaker who copes with the zombie apocalypse by shooting it on his camcorder and uploading the footage to the internet. Think *Cloverfield*... with zombies.'

Peter Bradshaw of the *Guardian* was less impressed and wrote in his review: 'The opening news-report sequence is very strong. But from there on in... well, what more is there to say about the zombie genre and its metaphors for our undead society?'

DID YOU KNOW?

Stephen King and Quentin Tarantino voiced characters in the movie. As George explained to Capone from Ain't It Cool News: 'In the end, we had a movie that had four voices on it – my girlfriend, me, the producer Peter Grunwald, and the editor. And we can't put the movie out with just four voices on it, so initially I called Stephen [King], he was the first guy. And I said: "Steve, I need this kind of preacher guy. Would you consider doing the voice?" And he said sure. We were able to do them all over the telephone because none of them required fidelity, because in the movie, they're all coming over some sort of electronic medium… Then we called Quentin [Tarantino], and we called Guillermo [del Toro] for the immigration perspective.'

E IS FOR...

THE EVIL DEAD (1981)

This was the first of three horror movies by Sam Raimi and produced by Bruce Campbell, Robert Tapert and Dino De Laurentiis. All three have the same hero, Ashley 'Ash' J Williams (Bruce Campbell) and the same enemy, the deadites (demon-possessed corpses). The *Necronomicon Ex Mortis* – written by the Dark Ones – also features in all three movies. It is, as the online film critic James Berardinelli explained in his review of the movie, 'a strange book whose pages are made out of human skin and whose writing is done in human blood. This is the *Necronomicon*, or the "Book of the

Dead", which "speaks of a spiritual presence – a thing of evil – that roams the forests and dark bowers of man's domain". It also includes incantations to raise demons.'

In the movie, Ash is a student who travels with four of his friends to an isolated cabin in the mountains of Tennessee. They expect to have a nice weekend enjoying the scenery but this all goes to pot when they find the Book of the Dead. They make the mistake of playing a tape they find in the cabin which is actually a recording of words that, spoken together, have a demonic power. In playing the tape they have resurrected demons!

Ash's sister Cheryl (Ellen Sandweiss) becomes the first person to be possessed by one of them. It hypnotises her and makes her go into the forest. The demon possesses the trees and rapes her. She manages to escape but when she tells the others what has happened they don't believe her. Ash decides that it would be best if he took her to the nearest town so she can spend the night there, but they have to turn back as the bridge they need to use is damaged.

Cheryl ends up dying and the demon that attacked her takes control of her body. She is no longer Ash's sister and is now a deadite. She uses a pencil to stab Linda (Betsy Baker) in the ankle and Scotty (Hal Delrich) locks her in the cellar after hitting her with the handle of an axe. They might have thought they would be safe with Cheryl unable to escape but another demon kills and possesses Shelly (Sarah York). The Shelly deadite attacks Scotty and this time he uses his axe to chop her into pieces. He thinks the best thing he can do is try to find a trail so they can leave the cabin and the woods. He doesn't care about Linda, he just wants to get out of there.

While he goes to look for a trail, Ash goes to see Linda but she too is possessed. Scotty comes back but he has been attacked by the demons who possessed the trees and is barely alive. He found the trail and tells Ash about it before he passes out. Ash manages to lock Linda outside but she returns as a deadite. Scotty dies, so Ash and Shelly are the only people from the group left alive. Ash is attacked by Linda but manages to stop her by stabbing her with a dagger. He knows he should dismember her so she can't come back, but he can't face using his chainsaw on his friend. He buries her but she rises from her grave and he ends up cutting her head off with the shovel he used to bury her.

When he goes back inside he sees that the cellar door is open so Cheryl is on the loose. He takes some extra shells for his shotgun and heads for Scotty and Shelly's bedroom as he thinks she's hiding in there. She is, and he shoots her as she tries to take his shotgun. She isn't affected by it and he will have to come up with another way of killing her. He makes sure both doors are blocked and then goes for more shells in the cellar.

Strange things are happening in the cellar; it is filling with blood and the recorder and other electrical devices start being powered on their own. He hears the voices of his friends telling him they are going to get him, but he tells the voices to shut up. He is thinking of Linda when Cheryl attacks him and he shoots her. A deadite Scotty then appears and attacks him but Ash manages to gouge his eyes out. As they struggle he notices that the Book of the Dead by the fireplace has started to burn, and so has Scotty. He realises that they are linked and that by burning the book he can stop the demons. He can't do anything about it, though, because Cheryl and Scotty are both attacking him. Scotty has him pinned to the floor and Cheryl is hitting him with a poker from the fireplace. However, he persists, and after using Linda's necklace he manages to knock the book into the fire, just as Cheryl is about to stick the poker through his chest.

The bodies of his possessed friends fall to pieces as the book is destroyed and the demons leave. It looks like Ash will be OK and he goes to leave, but the voice of an Unseen Evil can be heard as it heads for Ash. He screams and the credits roll.

Critics and horror fans loved *The Evil Dead* and the film has received rave reviews ever since its release. Martyn Glanville from the BBC gave it four out of five stars and said in his review: 'Shot on 16mm at an initial cost of $85,000 in 1979, it was finished two years later. *The Evil Dead* is a first film that easily surpasses other notorious horror debuts such as *The Last House on the Left* or *The Texas Chainsaw Massacre*. The influence of the Three Stooges on its comical creative trio of director Raimi, producer Robert Tapert and lead actor Bruce Campbell gives the film a playful but unsettling feel. While they would take this humour further in *Evil Dead II* and *Army of Darkness*, here it blends effectively with the squirming gore that gives the film its reputation. A pencil stabbed into an ankle is amusing in a Stooge-like way, but when its point repeatedly digs and gouges into the recipient's flesh, we're given enough time to contemplate our own ankle under attack and are left feeling appropriately horrified.'

Online critic James Berardinelli enjoyed the movie, giving it three out of four stars, but felt that not everyone would. He wrote: 'A strong stomach is required. If you can't take copious amounts of blood and gore, this is not your movie. Both *The Evil Dead* and *Evil Dead II* have enough vile-coloured liquids to fill a small swimming pool. Plus, there are assorted body parts (decapitated heads, bodiless hands, etc). Of course, the extreme nature of the gore isn't beside the point – it is the point. Raimi goes so far over the top in presenting these displays that they take on a campy, almost humorous appearance. It's impossible to take all this blood seriously. So, instead of being sickened, we're strangely amused – and this is all intentional. (In general in horror films, it's the little displays of blood – like a fingernail being pulled off – that cause the most discomfort. The more outrageous a display, the less likely it is to be taken seriously.)'

EVIL DEAD II (1987)

Six years after *The Evil Dead* came out, *Evil Dead II* hit the cinemas. Written by Sam Raimi and Scott Spiegel, it became a cult classic like its predecessor.

The movie starts with a retcon (retelling) of the first movie so that people who hadn't seen it would know what was going on. The story was altered slightly so that instead of five people spending the weekend in the cabin it had been just Ash and his girlfriend Linda. The movie had ended with an Unseen Evil entering Ash, but we learn 15 minutes in that the demon seemingly left his body at dawn. Ash knows he has to get as far away from the cabin as possible but he can't because the bridge has been damaged.

Meanwhile, Annie (Sarah Berry), the daughter of the man who found the Book of the Dead in the first place and recorded the message that caused the demons to appear, has arrived at the damaged bridge with Ed, her researcher boyfriend. They have found extra pages from the book and have hired Bobby Jo and Jake to show them another way of getting up to the cabin.

Ash is taking a nap but is woken up by piano music. Outside, the corpse of Linda (his dead girlfriend) is dancing. She disappears but her head appears on Ash's lap and attacks him. Her teeth sink into his right hand and nothing Ash does can make Linda release her grip. He goes to the shed outside and uses a vice to free his hand but Linda's headless body then appears and attacks him with his chainsaw. He manages to evade it and, to make sure he won't be seeing Linda again, he uses the chainsaw to obliterate her head.

When he gets back to the cabin he sees something that frightens him to the core. Something is on the rocking chair and the sight of it causes him to drop his shotgun. He tries to give himself a stern talking to in the mirror but his own reflection starts attacking him verbally and physically. After it disappears, his own hand starts using plates to attack him. It wants to cause permanent damage with a cleaver, but, before it can, Ash uses his chainsaw to chop it off. Even when it is separated from his body it doesn't die and Ash has to think of some way of stopping it. He traps it in a tin but it escapes and goes inside the cabin's wall. He uses his shotgun to try to blast it to smithereens but the walls start to spew blood everywhere. As quickly as the blood appeared it disappears, and Ash ends up on a chair that collapses. Items in the room start laughing at Ash and he joins in – he is no longer sane.

When Annie, Ed, Bobby Jo and Jake arrive, he initially thinks the four of them are more demons sent to torment him and fires his shotgun, which makes them think that he is a mad murderer. Annie had expected her parents to be in the cabin and thinks Ash must have killed them.

They lock him in the cellar but realise what is going on when they listen to a recording by Annie's father, the professor who found the book. Professor Knowby's wife Henrietta was possessed by a demon and he buried her in the cellar. She rises and attacks Ash but the others help to overpower her and lock her in the cellar. The demon isn't going to go down without a fight and tries to trick Annie into letting it out, but Ash intervenes. A demon then possesses Ed and Ash quickly gets an axe and kills him. They are then joined by the spirit of Professor Knowby, who says that the new pages will help them get rid of the evil dead permanently.

Bobby Jo makes a run for it when Ash's right hand grabs her hand but she can't escape. The demons possess the trees and kill her. When Ash and Annie look inside the book they see that the hero figure has a 'boomstick' and a chainsaw for a hand – Ash. Jake doesn't know that Bobby Jo is dead and wants them to go and look for her. The whole situation has messed with his mind; he picks up the shotgun and throws the new pages of the book into the cellar. Once outside, they find that Bobby Jo's trail has disappeared and a demon enters Ash. Ash attacks Jake, pushing him against a tree until he passes out. Annie runs for her life and Ash chases her back to the cabin. She takes the bone dagger and accidentally wounds Jake as he tries to get inside. She takes him in and locks the door so Ash can't get in. As she drags Jake to the cellar her mother Henrietta attacks him and finishes him off.

Ash manages to get in and just before he is about to kill Annie, he rips off her necklace and it reminds him of the necklace his girlfriend Linda used to have. He takes control of his body once more and convinces Annie that they can get rid of the evil dead together.

Annie helps him turn his chainsaw into a chainsaw hand by attaching it to the stump of his right arm. He is now ready for the job he needs to do but they must have those pages. He fights with Henrietta while Annie gets them, and it is a truly awful fight as the demon inside Henrietta is extremely strong. It looks like Henrietta is about to kill Ash but Annie manages to stop her in her tracks by singing a lullaby that her mother used to sing to her when she was growing up. Henrietta is distracted, which allows Ash to decapitate her and then shoot her in the head so there is no chance of the demon reanimating.

As Annie reads the text, a large, bloody head begins to form that has all the faces of the people the demons have possessed. Ash has to fight it until Annie's words cause a portal to open outside the cabin. They think the portal will just take the demons but it has so much power that it takes everything, from the trees to Ash's car, the Oldsmobile. Ash's possessed hand stabs Annie in the back with the dagger but she manages to say the final words before dying.

Ash is sucked through the portal and finds himself in the year 1300. He is accused of being a deadite by some knights but they realise he isn't when a winged demon appears. Ash blasts it in the head with his shotgun, killing it. The knights and the rest of the people think he is going to save them all, with one knight declaring: 'Hail he who hath fallen from the sky to deliver us from the terror of the deadites!' Ash can't believe that his nightmare still isn't over and he screams as the credits roll.

Many reviewers and critics felt that *Evil Dead II* was even better than the first movie and *Time* magazine later included it in its list of the 'Top Ten Movie Sequels Better than the Originals' (alongside *Terminator 2: Judgment Day*, *Tron: Legacy*, *The Bourne Ultimatum*, *The Empire Strikes Back*, *Star Trek II: The Wrath of Khan*, *Before Sunset*, *Bride of Frankenstein*, *Harry Potter and the Prisoner of Azkaban*, and *National Lampoon's Christmas Vacation*).

The magazine said: 'When director Sam Raimi got the chance to make a sequel for his cult hit *The Evil Dead*, he came up with a brilliant plan that would ensure that the next movie was as good (if not better) than the first. Instead of using another location for his horror movie or trying to brainstorm a new plot, Raimi basically remade that first film, except this time with a bigger budget and fewer rookie-filmmaker mistakes.

'It's hard to believe that the only surviving character of the first instalment Ash (Bruce Campbell) would return to the woods where his friends were brutally murdered by demons and rapist trees just a few years before. That illogic helps add to the campiness of this film, which showcases Raimi's ability to terrify the viewer and make them laugh out loud at the same time. While the first film took itself a little too seriously, *Evil Dead II* pokes fun at demon possession and evil enchantments without turning the movie into a farce. When your protagonist has a chainsaw for an arm, you know you're in for a treat.'

For the third in the trio of Evil Dead movies, and how it differed from *The Evil Dead* and *Evil Dead II*, see *Army of Darkness*.

F IS FOR...

FIDO (2006)

Fido is a social-satire zombie movie by Canadian director Andrew Currie, who wrote it with Robert Chomiak and Dennis Heaton. It stars Billy Connolly as Fido, K'Sun Ray as Timmy, Carrie-Anne Moss as Helen and Tim Blake Nelson as Mr Theopolis.

Fido is set in an alternative universe where the dead have become zombies because of a surge of radiation from outer space. Unaffected humans fought back against them in the Zombie Wars and won, forcing the zombies to be their slaves, but when the humans die they too become zombies, unless their bodies are cremated or beheaded. A government organisation called Zomcon is in charge of controlling the zombies, who are fitted with a special collar that controls their need for human flesh.

A housewife called Helen buys a zombie to help her around the house. Her son Timmy befriends it and calls it Fido. Her husband Bill has a phobia of zombies after fighting in the Zombie Wars but this doesn't stop Helen. Fido is easy to control until a fault develops in the collar and Fido kills their neighbour. Timmy manages to kill the neighbour when he returns as a zombie, but someone else gets bitten and before long there is a mini-outbreak of zombies. The family doesn't let on that Fido caused it.

When Zomcon investigates the disappearance of the neighbour, two local bullies are blamed. The bullies decide to hold Timmy and Fido hostage but Fido eventually frees himself and manages to find Helen. She is able to save her son from the now zombified bullies – Fido had killed them earlier and they have reanimated.

When the neighbour's corpse is found, it is revealed that Fido is the real murderer and he is removed by the Zomcon officials. He should be destroyed but Timmy finds out that he has been redeployed and is working in a factory controlled by Zomcon. With the help of Mr Theopolis, a former Zomcon employee, Timmy decides to try to free his friend but is captured by the evil security chief Mr Bottoms. He tries to have Timmy killed by forcing him into the 'wild zone', which is full of zombies roaming around looking for stranded humans to kill and eat. Bill arrives just in time and saves Timmy, but he is murdered by Mr Bottoms. Fido then kills Mr Bottoms and frees Timmy.

Helen has Bill decapitated at his funeral so he won't return as a zombie, as she knows he would have hated that. Fido returns to the family (minus his collar) and helps look after Helen and Bill's new baby when it arrives. Fido finds that smoking stops him wanting to kill people and eat them.

FIRST PLATOON (2011)

First Platoon is a horror comedy movie written and directed by Chris Gabriel, who is most famous for directing *Devotion* and *S4*. It stars Malcolm McDowell, Dale Dye and John Kassir, and its tagline is 'Making the World a Slightly Safer Place'.

A press release for the movie, scheduled for release in 2011, stated: '*First Platoon* is an homage to a genre virtually created by George Romero, and stays true to the classic zombie lore that diehard fans revere, while offering a fast-moving adventure with plenty of hilarity.'

DAN OLIVER

FLESHEATER (1988)

Written, directed, produced and edited by S William Hinzman, *FleshEater* is a zombie movie that had a budget of $60,000 and a tag line of 'He lived, he died, he's back, and he's hungry!' Hinzman also played the main role of FleshEater.

The movie centres around a group of teenagers who are taking a hayride in the countryside on Halloween. They pay the local farmer to take them to a secluded area of the forest and then arrange for him to pick them up after dark. They start drinking and having a good time together before couples start breaking off to be alone.

Meanwhile another farmer decides to remove an old tree stump near the group's party location. As he pulls it away using his tractor, he notices a large wooden box with what looks to be an ancient seal with a warning, telling him not to open it. The farmer ignores the warning and, as he opens the box, he releases a zombie called FleshEater.

The zombie eats him alive and the farmer turns into a zombie himself. Together they go hunting for the teenagers. FleshEater looks inside a barn and finds two of them. He kills them but two of their friends see what is happening and run for their lives. They quickly tell their other friends what has happened. The attacked teenagers turn into zombies so there are now four zombies after the others!

A girl is about to become the next victim when her shoulder is torn off but her boyfriend arrives during the attack and tries to save her. The remaining group seek sanctuary in an old farmhouse in the forest. They start boarding up the windows and doors to stop the zombies getting in and use the phone to ring the police, but the zombies rip the phone lines out before they get the chance to explain what is happening.

Two of the friends are stuck outside as they arrive later and the others won't let them in. They have already boarded the house up and don't want to risk it in case the zombies get in too. The two friends manage to get into the basement and stay there.

The girl with the injured shoulder dies and comes back as a zombie. The zombies manage to break into the house and kill everyone, apart from the two hiding in the basement. The teenagers reanimate into zombies and join FleshEater. Their next victim turns out to be a policeman who is sent to investigate what is going on. He manages to shoot two of the zombies but there are too many of them and he is eaten too.

The lucky teenagers who locked themselves in the basement eventually come out of hiding to find the policeman's corpse, still with his weapon. They take the gun and kill off his zombified body before fleeing for safety.

FleshEater rallies his new troops as they continue to kill people, their next victims being a family who are eaten alive in their home. The two surviving teenagers manage to make it to some stables and warn the owner of the terror that awaits him and his wife if they don't leave immediately. The owner goes home to get his wife, but there is already a zombie waiting for him and he is killed. The teenagers flee again and find a Halloween party in a barn but the partygoers shrug them off as pranksters. The couple hide in the barn's framework and the zombies soon arrive and set about killing everyone else.

The police in the area group together to attack the zombies and put a stop to them. They arm themselves and then go through the forest shooting every zombie they find. When they reach the barn they kill all the zombies, but the teenage couple who had managed to evade the zombies are shot and killed too because they are mistaken for zombies. The police burn all the bodies and think they have been successful, but FleshEater hasn't been killed. When a policeman decides to return to the barn he is eaten and reanimates…

DID YOU KNOW?

S William Hinzman played the cemetery zombie in *Night of the Living Dead*.

FLIGHT OF THE LIVING DEAD: OUTBREAK ON A PLANE (2007)

Flight of the Living Dead is an action horror movie directed by Scott Thomas, who wrote it with Mark Onspaugh. David Chisum played Truman, Kristen Kerr played Megan, Kevin J O'Connor played Frank and Richard Tyson played Paul. The tagline for the movie was 'Un-dead at 30,000 feet'.

Flight of the Living Dead begins with a group of crazy scientists on board a flight from Los Angeles to Paris. They are attempting to flee the pursuing CIA and they are transporting the coffin of their former work colleague, whose corpse is contaminated with a genetically modified virus. The virus is carried through the body in the form of fluid, and allows infected individuals to continue their actions no matter what. The CIA consider this to be a form of biological weapon.

The aircraft hits a storm and the turbulence allows the zombified corpse to slip out of the cargo hold. Two of the scientists go to check on the coffin but are killed by the zombie and then reanimate themselves. A zombie pandemic breaks out and the passengers are helpless, thousands of feet up in the sky with no chance of escaping. The virus allows the zombies to outperform what a normal human being is capable of. This becomes evident as the first zombie is able to carry out his massacre despite being thrown into one of the aircraft's engines.

The passengers struggle to take control of the flight but are told by officials on the ground that the plane will not be allowed to land at any airfield. Anna, Burrows, Frank, Paul and Megan are the only uninfected people left, and they need to make it clear to the fighter jet on their tail that not all members on board have been savaged, otherwise they will be shot down. They secure an MP5 submachine gun and attempt to kill off all the zombified passengers, but during the fight both Paul and Anna are bitten.

Burrows and Frank make it to the cockpit of the plane and Frank kills the co-pilot, who is a zombie. Burrows and Frank are able to signal that they have now gained control of the aircraft by moving the plane from side to side. However, although the fighter jet has aborted its attempt to blow up the plane, the first missile it sent is still enough to damage the aircraft.

The plane is going to crash and Burrows and Frank struggle to steer it. It crashes into a mountainside close to Las Vegas and the pilot reanimates after impact and becomes a zombie. Burrows manages to kill it with the MP5, and the survivors head for Las Vegas – not knowing that four zombies are following them.

G IS FOR...

GALLOWWALKER (2010)

Gallowwalker was directed by Andrew Goth, most famous for directing the horror movie *Cold and Dark*, who also wrote the script along with Joanne Reay. Its tagline was 'Live by the gun. Die by the gun. Come back for more.' The movie stars Wesley Snipes as Aman, Riley Smith as Fabulos, Tanit Phoenix as Angel and Kevin Howarth as Kansa.

The movie centres on a crazed killer with a gun. Aman was cursed from birth and every single one of his innocent victims is brought back to life as a zombie. He is soon being tailed by a lynch mob of these flesh-hungry creatures, led by Kansa. In his panicked attempt to keep himself from becoming their war trophy Aman recruits a sidekick by the name of Fabulos to help him in his battle.

GANGS OF THE DEAD (2006)

Directed by Duane Stinnett and written by him with Krissann Shipley, *Gangs of the Dead* was originally given the title *Last Rites*. It stars Enrique Almeida as Santos, Howard Alonzo as Jerome, Reggie Bannister as Mitchell and Stephen Basilone as O'Bannon.

The movie shows a zombie apocalypse set in the tough streets of downtown Los Angeles. The ever-present feuds between two drug-dealing gangs and the city's police department are blown into a whole new proportion when a meteorite riddled with zombie-creating spores hits the infamous city. The gangs face a new enemy – flesh-hungry zombies – and the toughest have no choice but to join forces with the Los Angeles Police Department.

GARDEN OF THE DEAD (1974)

Garden of the Dead (called *Tomb of the Undead* in some countries) was directed by John Hayes, who is mainly a

B-movie director. It was written by John Jones and Daniel Cady, and the latter also produced the movie. Duncan McLeod plays Dr Saunders, John Dullaghan plays Sergeant Burns, John Dennis plays Jablonski and Marland Proctor plays Paul Johnson.

In this movie, experiments are being conducted on inmates in an American prison. Two inmates decide to take more of the drug because they think it will get them high. They manage to steal the drug but after taking it they decide to try to escape. While trying to make a run for it, they are spotted by the prison guards who shoot them dead. The prisoners are then buried in the prison graveyard, but the men rise from their graves as zombies and kill everyone who crosses their path. They want more of the drug and will kill to get their hands on it!

THE GHOST GALLEON (1974)

The Ghost Galleon – also known as *El Buque Maldito* – is a Spanish movie, directed and written by Amando de Ossorio. Maria Perschy played Lillian, Jack Taylor played Howard, Bárbara Rey played Noemi and Carlos Lemos played Professor Grüber.

The movie starts with two models on a mission to create a dramatic publicity stunt for a new car launch, but after reporting a ship of ghosts they go missing in the fog covering the sea. They have been captured by a passing ghost galleon occupied by zombies who are Satan-worshipping knights. A search party is sent to find them and when the rescuers find the ancient vessel they see its ghoulish occupants. Will they become heroes and save the captured girls or will they too become entrapped?

H IS FOR...

HIDE AND CREEP (2004)

Hide and Creep is a comedy horror movie directed by Chuck Hartsell and Chance Shirley. The script was written by Chance and they based the movie on a short film they had done together called *Birthday Call*. The movie follows what happens when a town is attacked by aliens and zombies at the same time. A government agent is sent to investigate a UFO sighting and is bitten (and killed) by a zombie who rises from its grave. The movie then splits into four stories.

In the first story three men are at their hunting lodge when they come under attack from a group of zombies.

They don't have any guns so they decide to run into the woods and split up in the hope that they will be able to get away safely. Two of them make it back to the lodge with guns. One of the two tries to get hold of the sheriff but is told that he is out and that the best thing to do is shoot the zombies in the head. The pair set about shooting any zombies that come into range.

The third man returns but he has been bitten. He lies and says he got his injuries from running into a tree, and the three men decide to leave the lodge and head for the town centre. The bitten man soon starts to change and his friends have no choice but to kill him. One of the men goes into a grocery store but is killed by the people inside because they think he is a zombie. The remaining man goes into a strip club and is confronted by strippers who have turned into zombies. They are scared of the dark and he decides that he must get the word out, so he rings the local radio station.

He then goes home and picks up his two daughters, who have been fighting the zombies on their own. They need to get out of town fast. He lets a woman who works at the police station and her ex-boyfriend travel with them in their car and things are going well until his youngest daughter says she is hungry and attacks him. The car swerves and it looks like they are going to die.

The second story doesn't feature zombies but focuses on a man who was abducted by aliens.

In the third story a preacher is bitten by a zombie but tries to carry on as normal. He is asked to give a sermon to comfort the people in the town and he agrees. Before the sermon he steals some liquor to help him cope with the pain he is feeling because of the bite. The woman who owns the liquor tries to stop him but he attacks her. He hates the fact that he now desires blood and when he gives the sermon he does the opposite of what he was supposed to do. Instead of comforting the people, he starts saying it is the end of the world. A zombie enters the church but he kills it before it can attack any of his congregation. He asks God to forgive him and then shoots himself in the head.

The fourth story sees a man called Chuck, who owns a video store, come under attack. Chuck kills the zombie by bashing it over the head with a video recorder, which then ejects *Night of the Living Dead*. He tries to contact the sheriff but he's out of town until Monday, so he rings his mum for advice. She tells him how to get blood off his shirt. He then decides to dump the zombie's body at the police station, leaving a note with his name and number so the sheriff can call him.

Chuck next gets chatting to a man called Chris and goes with him to try to find the police secretary's car, which has been taken by the government agent. They find the agent but not the car and go back to the station. Chuck volunteers to man the police station while the others go on another search for the missing car. While he's in charge he decides to smoke some marijuana and watch a college football match on TV.

Chuck isn't happy when the news comes on instead of the match. He doesn't seem to care that his town is being invaded by zombies. The newsreader rings the police station asking for an update but Chuck isn't interested. He tells him he isn't a police officer and asks for the football match to be put on. Eventually he tells the newsreader what he knows about the zombies just to shut him up. The news broadcast continues so Chuck decides to listen to the radio. He finds out that the zombies are scared of the dark so decides he will stay in the police station until nightfall. The match is finally shown on TV and he decides to watch it before making his escape.

HOCUS POCUS (1993)

Hocus Pocus is a Disney film starring Bette Midler (Winnie), Sarah Jessica Parker (Sarah) and Kathy Najimy (Mary) as three sister witches who were killed in 1693 but return on Halloween 1993. They want to absorb the life power from a little girl called Dani but her brother Max and his love interest Allison won't let them. They steal the witches' spell book with the help of a black cat who used to be a boy called Thackery Binx. He was turned into a cat by the witches in 1693 when he tried to save his sister. As the trio and the cat try to escape, the witches chase them all over town.

The witches summon a zombie, a former lover of Winnie called Billy, to help them. He rises from his grave in the cemetery and at first helps the witches but then decides that he will help the children. As he tries to protect them, Winnie knocks his head off. Dani goes to retrieve his head but Winnie grabs her. The cat attacks Winnie, which makes her drop the potion she needs. Max drinks it and Winnie is so angry that she takes Max and starts draining the life from him. He manages to fight back and she lands on the ground. Because they are in the cemetery, and she is forbidden from standing on hallowed ground, she turns to stone. As the sun rises all three witches explode, as their time on earth has run out.

Billy is a different type of zombie because he is a good zombie. He is also intelligent, brave and heroic. He isn't interested in eating brains, just saving the children. He had died after Winnie caught him fooling around with her sister Sarah. She wanted to punish him for betraying her, so she poisoned him and then sewed his mouth together.

The actor chosen to play Billy was Doug Jones, who is most famous for playing Abe Sapien in the Hellboy movies. It took Doug two and a half hours to get into his costume and have his make-up applied every day. The make-up artist who oversaw the whole process was

Tony Gardner, who went into detail about what Doug had to do on Doug's official website. 'Doug wears a make-up appliance of a paper-thin foam latex that covers everything from his ears forward and his entire neck. In addition, he wears a full body suit, long gloves with acrylic extensions on the ends of his fingers to add length, a ratty wig and big shoes with fake toes coming through them. The intention was to create a character who would walk a fine line between grotesque – because he has been dead for quite some time – and handsome. He is regal, an aristocrat, but very dead.

'We exaggerated Doug's physical features... he has a small nose and a very narrow face onto which we could place the latex, reshaping his face, with hollowed cheeks and deep-set eyes. Kenny [Ortega, the director] wanted him to look innocent, a Bambi-look, with doe eyes. Doug's eyes are very expressive and stand out with the make-up. Underneath his costume he wears the body suit with all the textural details of a zombie, exaggerated bone structure at the knees and elbows.'

HOUSE OF THE DEAD (2003)

House of the Dead was a zombie movie based on a Sega arcade game and directed by a German director called Uwe Boll. Uwe has directed many movies based on video games including *Alone in the Dark*, *BloodRayne* and *Far Cry*. The cast were relatively unknown, although Erica Durance, who played one of the girls, went on to play Lois Lane in the TV series *Smallville*.

The movie starts with two young lads, Simon and Greg, and three girls, Alicia, Cynthia and Karma, wanting to go to an island rave. When they go to catch the boat that will take them there, they find that it has already left. They don't want to miss out so they ask two men, Victor and Salish, to take them there. A cop called Casper warns them that one of the men is a smuggler but they don't care – they just want to get to the party.

When they arrive at the island they are surprised that they can't see anyone and the place is a mess. Simon sets out with Alicia and Karma to try to find the partygoers. Greg and Cynthia stay behind and start kissing but Greg needs to relieve himself. He goes to pee but while he's gone some zombies arrive and kill Cynthia. Elsewhere on the island, Simon, Alicia and Karma find three people hiding inside an old house. Rudy, Hugh and Liberty explain what happened earlier. They had been enjoying the party when zombies ambushed them and killed everyone else. The six of them decide to go back to get Greg and Cynthia, and then leave on Victor and Salish's boat. Meanwhile Victor and Salish have no idea what danger surrounds them and when Salish goes for a walk through the forest he is killed.

When the group from the old house make it to the rave site, they see Cynthia but she has changed into a zombie. She kills Hugh before they can stop her and Casper ends up shooting her. They need to get off the island as soon as they can, but their means of escape, the boat, is crawling with zombies. They have to think of something else so they split up. Greg and Casper go for help but Greg is then killed. Thankfully Victor knows where some guns are hidden and soon everyone has a weapon. They are going to have to fight if they are to survive. They go back to the old house and find more zombies. Casper and Liberty are killed but the others make it inside safely.

Victor is distraught when he sees that his friend Salish is now a zombie. He's had enough and blows himself up. The rest of the group go to a laboratory in the house but the zombies are desperately trying to get in and the door won't hold for long. Karma sees a trap door and knows they have no choice but to go down it. Alicia and Rudy go too but Simon stays behind. He causes a huge explosion, which kills him and the nearby zombies.

The other three continue down underground tunnels but come under attack again. Karma sacrifices herself so Alicia and Rudy can escape but they are soon in the company of Castillo, the man behind the zombies. He is immortal thanks to a special serum with which he injected himself, and he is wearing Greg's face as a mask. Alicia tries to fight him but he stabs her. Rudy manages to cut his head off but Castillo still isn't dead – his body moves without its head. It grabs Rudy and starts strangling him. In her last moments Alicia manages to crush the head, which kills him, but she too dies. Quick-thinking Rudy gives her some of the serum so she is restored to full fitness and they are both rescued by federal agents.

House of the Dead failed to emulate the success of the arcade game. Critics hated it and it featured in the Internet Movie Database's 'Bottom 100' list and the website GT Countdown's 'Top 10 Worst Video Game Movies'. On Rotten Tomatoes its score was just 4 out of a possible 100.

Jamie Russell of the BBC wrote in his review that it was 'one of the worst zombie movies ever made', adding: 'Just when it looked like zombies were cool again, this truly pointless adaptation of the plot-lite *House of the Dead* videogame threatens to send them back to the undertakers. A group of fresh-faced kids (led by Jonathan Cherry) find themselves stuck on a deserted island and pursued by fleet-footed zombies after an illegal party brings corpses back from the grave. It's inept, inane and it sucks like an airplane toilet. It's bad enough to make *Resident Evil: Apocalypse* look like *Night of the Living Dead*.'

Linda Cook from the *Quad-City Times* seemed to agree: 'At first, I was riveted by its awfulness. Then, about 20 minutes later, I just wanted to go home.'

One of the few positive reviews was from the IGN Movies website. Their review gave it three out of five stars and stated: 'Like the game, the film is a fun romp through zombified excess, spiced up with generous doses of B-movie flair, rotting flesh hysteria, and mock subliminality. While not as technically brilliant as some zombie fare, *HotD* more than makes up for this lack in terms of sheer heart. Sure, it's a low-budget venture, but it doesn't feel forced or contrived, but rather revels in its low-budget restraints. That is to say it's not a slick Hollywood film masking as low-budget fare. Nor is it low-budget fare trying desperately to be slick Hollywood fodder. It's just an unabashed B-movie that does an incredibly decent job with a limited budget, unknown cast, and routine storyline.'

Zombie fans were unimpressed but the movie did make a profit, which was quite remarkable considering how badly it scored in reviews.

MOVIE MISTAKES

When they have the gunfight on the boat, the zombie with the net on his back reappears and is killed more than four times.

When Rudy falls off the bridge it is his right hand that is impaled on the nail, but in later scenes it is his left hand that is bandaged.

When Greg is being chased in the woods you can see the springboard that the zombie actor needed to be able to leap so high.

I IS FOR...

I AM LEGEND (2007)

When Richard Matheson published his novel *I Am Legend* in 1954, he helped to shape the way zombies would be depicted from then on. It was a horror novel set in the future and the Los Angeles it portrayed was full of zombie bloodsucking creatures. This type of zombie has been used in movies, TV dramas and computer games ever since. The book also showed a zombie apocalypse on a worldwide level caused by a disease and was used as the basis for four movies. *The Last Man on Earth* came out in 1964, *The Omega Man* in 1971, and *I Am Legend* and *I Am Omega* both came out in 2007.

The novel tells the story of Robert Neville, the only man left in Los Angeles who hasn't been transformed by the disease. He is immune to it; he has been bitten by an infected member of the undead but it just made him ill for a time. He wants to understand what happened and, if possible, research a cure. Robert struggles to cope but keeps on going. He has a routine: he tries to make his home as habitable as possible in the day, he gets rid of the undead corpses by burning them, and he tests the myths about vampires to keep himself safe. He knows they hate the smell of garlic, and that some vampires are repelled by crucifixes but others aren't. He tests running water, wooden stakes… and over the years he manages to kill thousands of the vampire-like creatures.

At night they attack his home, wanting him to come out so they can get at him. One of them used to be his friend Ben, but he has no friends any more. He tests his theory about crucifixes on Ben because Ben was a Jew before he changed. His theory is right: the crucifix doesn't repel him but the Talmud does.

Robert feels so helpless that he turns to alcohol, but he does manage to find out how the disease started, and that there is a particular strain of bacteria that infected people. What he doesn't realise is that there are two types of infected people: those who are undead and others who are being used as living hosts.

One day he comes across a woman who seems to be

unaffected like him. Maybe he isn't the last person alive after all. He isn't sure Ruth can be trusted and kidnaps her so he can find out more about her. He finds it hard to believe what she tells him because it has been so long since he's had contact with another human being. He can't understand why she doesn't want to kill the creatures like he does but they get closer as time passes.

One night he finds Ruth is leaving him, but after a heart-to-heart they sleep together. Robert wants her to take a blood test so he can double-check that she isn't infected, and she agrees, but she knows she is. The second the results are revealed she knocks him unconscious and makes her escape. She knows she owes him an apology, so she writes a note detailing her real story and to explain the fact that she is one of the infected who are living hosts. She is part of a group who have learned to spend time in the sunlight and are determined to do the things they used to do as humans.

Robert has become an enemy of Ruth and her comrades without even realising it. He had always thought that there was only one kind of creature and he has been killing both kinds. Because of this they despise him and want to capture him, so they sent in Ruth to make him drop his guard.

When Robert reads this he is understandably shocked but he ignores Ruth's request for him to get out while he can. He stays put and is soon captured by them. They plan on killing him but Ruth doesn't want him to die. She has seen the real Robert and tries to help him escape, but she realises her plan has failed. She gives him some pills that will help make his execution easier on him. Robert knows his death is imminent. They kiss and he asks her to make sure that the new society being created is compassionate and not heartless.

When he sees the creatures outside waiting for his death he realises that they hate and fear him as much as he hated and feared them in the beginning. It is the end for him and the human race. He takes the pills and as he dies he thinks: '[I am] a new superstition entering the unassailable fortress of forever. I am legend.'

In its review of the book, the Geeks of Doom website wrote: 'What at first may appear to be a horror pulp story to be read under the covers then forgotten is nothing short of an astonishing analysis of not only then-current issues, but an examination that can be re-interpreted and used as a magnifying glass for any political or social strife. Cinema may be able to catch a glimmer of what Matheson brought to the page, but the story just cannot be translated to another medium as it stands. *I Am Legend* remains a classic and essential piece of modern literature for a reason, and it is nothing short of a masterpiece.'

Stephen King was greatly influenced by *I Am Legend* and wrote the foreword to a new edition published in

2006. He wrote: 'In the early 1950s, when the *Weird Tales* magazine was dying its slow death and Robert Bloch, horror's greatest writer at the time, had turned to psychological tales (and Fritz Leiber had fallen oddly silent) and the genre was languishing in the horse latitudes, Richard Matheson came like a bolt of pure ozone lightning. He single-handedly regenerated a stagnant genre, rejecting the conventions of the pulps that were already dying, incorporating sexual impulses and images into his work as Theodore Sturgeon had already begun to do in his science fiction, and writing a series of gut-bucket short stories.

'What do I remember about them? I remember what they taught me: the same thing that rock's most recent regenerator, Bruce Springsteen, articulates in one of his songs, no retreat, baby, no surrender. I remember that Matheson would never give ground. When you thought it had to be over, that your nerves couldn't stand any more, that was when Matheson turned on the afterburners. He wouldn't quit. He was relentless.'

Dan Schneider wrote in his review for *The International Writer's Magazine*: 'Despite having vampires in it, [the book] is not a novel on vampires, nor even a horror nor sci-fi novel at all, in the deepest sense. Instead, it is perhaps the greatest novel written on human loneliness. It far surpasses Daniel Defoe's *Robinson Crusoe* in that regard. Its insights into what it is to be human go far beyond genre, and is all the more surprising because, having read his short stories – which range from competent but simplistic, to having classic "Twilight Zone twists" [he was a major contributor to the original TV series] – there is nothing within those short stories that suggests the supreme majesty of the existential masterpiece *I Am Legend* was aborning.'

George A Romero was also greatly influenced by the novel when he was writing the script for *Night of the Living Dead*, as he admitted at the time: 'I had written a short story, which I basically had ripped off from a Richard Matheson novel called *I Am Legend*.'

Many people believe that he was influenced by the first movie based on the novel too. *Last Man on Earth* saw Robert with a different surname – he was Robert Morgan – but the main story was the same. The script was actually written by Richard Matheson himself with three other writers, but Richard wasn't happy when changes were made and he decided not to have his name in the credits. Instead he chose the pseudonym Logan Swanson. The movie was released in 1964.

Seven years later came *The Omega Man*. Robert Neville was played by Charlton Heston but Richard Matheson was not involved with the script at all and this movie was very different from the novel. The scriptwriters decided to use biological weapons as the reason why people were wiped out, and a lot of the plot was altered too. There was no Ruth, for example.

In 2007 two movies based on the novel were released. *I Am Omega* is set in Los Angeles but the main character is called Renchard. He has to help a woman called Brianna escape a city in which he has set bombs to go off in 24 hours, in the hope of killing as many of the cannibalistic humans as possible. He doesn't want to help her at first but he has no choice when two armed men arrive and demand that he does. Brianna is the only person who has the cure to the virus in her blood so she is irreplaceable. They save her but one of the men, Vincent, betrays them and shoots Renchard. He takes Brianna as his hostage because he isn't ready for the world to change. Renchard manages to get enough strength back to rescue her and he kills Vincent. Together Renchard and Brianna will develop the cure.

This movie was made on a low budget and went straight to video. It was rushed out because the movie's distributor – The Global Asylum – wanted it to come out a month before *I Am Legend* hit the cinemas. The company specialises in releasing movies to video that benefit from the success of big Hollywood blockbusters. For instance, when *Snakes on a Plane* came out in 2006 they released *Snakes on a Train*. When *The Da Vinci Code* came out they released *The Da Vinci Treasure*. *I Am Omega* would never have been made if Warner Bros hadn't decided to make *I Am Legend*.

The biggest adaptation to date, *I Am Legend*, came out on 14 December 2007. Warner Bros had wanted to make a movie based on Richard Matheson's novel for a long time and had started planning it back in 1994. The movie was directed by Francis Lawrence, who went on to direct the Robert Pattinson movie *Water for Elephants*. He is best known for directing music videos, and was the man behind Lady Gaga's 'Bad Romance', Beyoncé's 'Rule the World (Girls)' and Britney Spears' 'Circus' videos. Will Smith was the actor chosen to play Robert Neville.

For this movie the decision was made to have a virus that was meant to cure cancer cause the devastation. The infected in this movie are different from those in the novel as they are not as intelligent, but they are sensitive to light and want blood. The time was brought up to date: instead of being set in the 1970s, the movie was set in 2009 and 2012. The project had a budget of $159 million and when they shot the scene at Brooklyn Bridge they spent $5 million on it. To date it has made more than $585 million.

In this movie Robert Neville is a lieutenant in the military and a scientist who specialises in viruses and the different ways in which they can be used. His daughter and wife were killed in December 2009 when they were travelling in a helicopter to escape the chaos caused by the genetically engineered virus – the Krippen Virus – that was supposed to be a cure for cancer but wiped out more than 5 billion people worldwide.

Three years pass and Robert is living a lonely

existence as the last man in New York. The virus might not have killed everyone but 588 million survivors were affected and turned into bald, zombie predators who are cannibalistic and need blood. These super-fast creatures take the name Darkseekers. Only 12 million people proved immune to the Krippen Virus and they became the Darkseekers' prey. Robert hasn't seen people like himself for a long time. In the daytime he can move around New York relatively freely as the Darkseekers can't stand UV light. Some of his former friends are now Darkseekers and he is determined to find a cure.

Robert's life revolves around performing experiments on rats and Darkseekers who have the virus, sending out radio messages in case there is another survivor listening, and hunting wild deer for food. He records his own video diary too. He is incredibly lonely and talks to mannequins as if they are real people. His only companion is a German Shepherd dog he found, called Sam.

Robert needs another specimen and successfully captures a female Darkseeker using a snare trap. Robert expects a new serum he has developed to change the female Darkseeker, but when he tries it it doesn't work. The next day he himself falls victim to a snare trap when he sees one of his mannequins has been moved. He loses consciousness for a time and, when he wakes up, he is attacked by infected wild dogs as he tries to escape. Sam is badly injured and Robert tries desperately to save her life. He injects her with some serum thinking that might heal her but it doesn't – it makes her attack him. He has to strangle his one and only friend before she causes him permanent damage.

Without Sam his life seems pointless and Robert decides to commit suicide, with the aim of killing as many of the Darkseekers as possible at the same time. He sets off in his car, which he has rigged up with UV light, and manages to kill many Darkseekers before he is overpowered. It looks like he will soon be dead but out of nowhere a woman called Anna and a young boy called Ethan come to his rescue. They have been listening to his messages on the radio and wanted to help. They take him back to his home and explain that they are planning to go to Bethel in Vermont because there are others like them there. They don't realise that they should have covered their scents before going to his house, because now the Darkseekers can find them. Up until then Robert had always managed to keep the location of his house a secret.

The Darkseekers want Robert dead and they attack his home. He tries to force them back using UV worklights but they manage to break them, so he uses claymore mines. This works, but there are so many that he can't stop them all and he ends up being attacked by the alpha male Darkseeker. Robert is able to fight him off but he realises that the alpha male was just sent to distract him so a hole could be made in the roof to allow more of the Darkseekers to get in.

Robert saves Anna and Ethan and together they go into the laboratory, which is the safest part of the house. The Darkseeker female that Robert captured is there too and the serum seems to be working as she becomes more humanlike. Robert knows that they will be able to survive for only a little bit longer as the Darkseekers are hitting the plexiglass walls that surround them and they will break through eventually. He has to save Anna and Ethan, so he decides to sacrifice himself and the female Darkseeker. He lets his friends into a secret coal chute at the back of the laboratory and passes them a vial containing the blood of the Darkseeker female so they can take the cure to the other survivors. Once they are safe he uses a hand grenade to blow up himself and the surrounding Darkseekers.

Anna and Ethan manage to make it to the other survivors in Vermont and hand over the vial. Anna says in her voice-over: 'In 2009, a deadly virus burned through our civilisation, pushing humankind to the edge of extinction. Dr Robert Neville dedicated his life to the discovery of a cure and the restoration of humanity. On 9 September 2012, at approximately 8.49pm, he discovered that cure. And at 8.52, he gave his life to defend it. We are his legacy. This is his legend. Light up the darkness.'

Will Smith loved filming the movie, despite its challenges. He explained to Collider.com: 'Shooting in New York, especially something on this level, is difficult. I would say that percentage-wise it's the most amounts of middle fingers I've ever received in my career. I was like, I'm used to people liking me – when I come to town it's fun [laughs] – so I thought "middle fingers"? I was starting to think "F-you" was my name [laughs].

'We shut down six blocks of Fifth Avenue on a Monday morning. That was probably poor logistics, which was poor planning. You realise that you have never actually seen an empty shot of New York. When we were doing it, it's chilling to walk down the middle of Fifth Avenue. There is never an opportunity to walk down the middle of Fifth Avenue. At two o'clock in the morning on Sunday you can't walk down the middle of Fifth Avenue. What happened is that it just created such a creepy energy.

'There are iconic buildings, there is a shot in the movie with the UN, there is Broadway, and it puts such an eerie, icky kind of feeling on the movie when you see those shots. Logistically it was a nightmare, but it absolutely created something that you can't do with green screen, and you can't do shooting another city instead of New York.'

When journalist Kam Williams from NewsBlaze.com asked if he had read the novel and watched the other movies, he admitted that he had. 'Yeah, I looked at both of them. And there are a couple of versions of the book, also. The idea of being alone and the fear of the dark is such a primal concept. Every four-year-old has thought about being separated from their family, and being alone, and it being dark, and what comes out of the dark. So, to me, the idea, in general, is in the collective unconscious. We're all keyed into these fears. As for the other film versions, I felt we would be able to bring something new with this film because in the past there's never been this level of technology available to support the weight of this story.'

DID YOU KNOW?

Before Will Smith signed up to play Robert, Tom Cruise, Mel Gibson and Michael Douglas were considered for the movie.

I SPIT ON YOUR RAVE (2010)

A British comedy horror movie, *I Spit on Your Rave* was filmed at the Big Chill Festival in August 2009. It stars Noel Fielding, who is most famous for playing Vince Noir in *The Mighty Boosh*, as the zombie king.

The movie is set in 2018 and the world is full of zombies after a zombie apocalypse occurred during the

London Olympics in 2012. The zombies can't eat humans anymore because they are extinct, so to cheer them up the zombie king decides to put on a zombie music festival.

One of the aims of the movie was to break a world record for the largest number of zombies captured on camera. The organisers asked festival-goers at the Big Chill to come dressed as zombies and they didn't disappoint. Officially 4,026 people took part, but organisers estimate that many more came as zombies but didn't fill out a form to be counted officially.

I WALKED WITH A ZOMBIE (1943)

I Walked with a Zombie is a horror movie directed by Jacques Tourneur which came out in 1943. It has become a zombie movie classic and in 2007 it was included in *Stylus* magazine's list of the 'Best Zombie Movies of All Time'. The movie was produced and written by Val Lewton, who worked with scriptwriters Inez Wallace, Ardel Wray and Curt Siodmak. They used Charlotte Brontë's *Jane Eyre* for inspiration and many elements from the novel were included in the final script.

The story tells what happens to a Canadian nurse called Betsy (Frances Dee) who is hired by a man called Paul Holland (Tom Conway) to care for his wife Jessica.

They live on the island of Saint Sebastian in the Caribbean. Their home is Fort Holland and it is revealed that it was the Hollands who brought slaves to Saint Sebastian.

Betsy meets Wesley, who is Paul's alcoholic half-brother, and he tells her about their mother. Later that night Betsy hears a woman crying and decides to go and find her. She crosses the courtyard and is about to climb the tower when she is attacked by the sleepwalking Jessica. Betsy's patient is like a ghost and her screams quickly bring Paul to her rescue and he takes his wife away.

It turns out that the woman crying was not in distress and Paul explains that it was a maid called Alma. She comes from a family who were slaves and they do things the opposite way round: they cry when a new baby is born and are happy when someone dies. Jessica's doctor explains that her sleepwalking is caused by an untreatable tropical fever and nothing can be done about it. Betsy discovers another explanation when she bumps into a drunk called Sir Lancelot on her day off. He sings a song that explains that Jessica had an affair with Wesley, Paul wouldn't let her go, and that is why she is shocked all the time. When Wesley arrives he apologises for what the drunk has been saying.

Later on Betsy finally gets to meet Paul and Wesley's mother, Mrs Rand, who is a doctor. While she is talking to her she can hear someone singing:

Her eyes are empty and she cannot talk,
And a nurse has come to make her walk.
The brothers are lonely and the nurse is young
And now you must see that my song is sung.

Betsy goes back to the Fort and witnesses Paul and Wesley arguing. Later, she hears Paul playing the piano and goes to him. He apologises for bringing her to Saint Sebastian and confesses that he may be to blame for the way Jessica is. Betsy hates to see Paul like this and decides that she must find a way of curing Jessica. She has grown to love Paul, even though she hasn't known him for long, and wants to help him.

Betsy thinks that giving Jessica insulin might help her but it doesn't work. Alma tells her about a voodoo priest who helped a woman with a similar condition but Paul's mother doesn't seem too keen. Betsy is willing to try anything and takes Jessica to the houmfort (where the voodoo priest and his worshippers meet). Getting there is no easy feat and they have to go past some crossroads guarded by a zombie, but when they finally arrive Betsy discovers that one of the voodoo priests is Paul's mother!

Mrs Rand had become a voodoo priest so she could help the people with medicine that they might not have accepted otherwise – she uses voodoo to win their trust. She tells Betsy that there is no way Jessica can be cured. While they talk the worshippers are watching Jessica in her trance-like state. One of them decides to use a sword to see if she is a zombie and they come to the conclusion that she is. Betsy takes her home but the worshippers want Jessica. They won't let up and the white people on the island start to feel extremely threatened. They suggest that Jessica should be admitted to a mental asylum on Saint Thomas.

The other voodoo priest, Sabreur, sends a man to kidnap Jessica but Mrs Rand manages to warn him off. Paul thinks that it would be better if Betsy went back to Canada before he does the same thing to her that he did to Jessica. Betsy can't see how he could abuse her or belittle her and wants to stay.

Hours later they are visited by a doctor who reveals that there is going to be an official inquiry into Jessica's state, and Wesley is pleased because he thinks his brother will get the blame. Their mother quickly sets them straight when she explains that Jessica is no longer human, she is a zombie. Jessica had been planning on running away with Wesley and Mrs Rand put a curse on her to stop her. She was temporarily possessed by a voodoo god who transformed Jessica into a zombie.

The doctor, Betsy and Paul can't believe what Mrs Rand is saying and think she is making it up. They don't think Jessica is a zombie because she isn't dead – her heart is still beating. But Wesley does believe her and wants to free Jessica from her zombie state. He asks Betsy about helping Jessica to die properly but Betsy refuses.

The voodoo priest Sabreur takes a voodoo doll to represent Jessica and uses it to make her leave the Fort. He also controls Wesley and has him follow her with an arrow. When the priest stabs the doll, Wesley stabs Jessica. Wesley then takes the body of the woman he loved into the sea and drowns. Their bodies are discovered and taken back to the Fort.

DID YOU KNOW?

Stylus magazine's 'Best Zombie Movies of All Time' were:

Dawn of the Dead (George Romero, 1978)
28 Days Later (Danny Boyle, 2002)
Day of the Dead (George Romero, 1985)
Dead Alive (Peter Jackson, 1992)
I Walked with a Zombie (Jacques Tourneur, 1943)
Night of the Living Dead (George Romero, 1968)
The Return of the Living Dead (Dan O'Bannon, 1985)
Deathdream (Bob Clark, 1974)
Shaun of the Dead (Edgar Wright, 2004)
Pet Sematary (Mary Lambert, 1989)

I, ZOMBIE: THE CHRONICLES OF PAIN (1998)

I, Zombie: The Chronicles of Pain was a movie written, directed and produced by Andrew Parkinson. He is best known for writing and directing *Dead Creatures*, *Venus Drowning* and *Little Deaths*.

At the start of the movie we learn that Mark (Giles Aspen) was supposed to be meeting up with his girlfriend Sarah (Ellen Softley) but preferred to search for moss samples instead. As he makes his way down a path to a farmhouse he sees an old car and when he goes inside he finds an injured man and a woman in pain. She screams and he decides he needs to take her to safety. He picks her up but she bites him, and he runs away as fast as he can. He collapses in a field but when he wakes he manages to make it home. His body changes and he becomes a zombie.

Mark can't live his old life and decides to run away. He doesn't want to kill people and at first he manages to resist the urge to kill and to eat flesh, but eventually he does kill a camper as his zombie side takes control. Sarah has no idea that Mark is a zombie and decides to get an investigator to try to hunt him down.

However much Mark hates killing, he has to do it again. His bite wound is becoming worse and after not eating flesh for almost a week he knows he has to feed again. He records what he is going through and how he is adapting to his new life. He knocks his victims out with chloroform before devouring them.

Time passes and Sarah meets someone else. One night she goes to the door after Mark rings her doorbell. He uses the chloroform on her and takes her back inside. He still loves her deep down and wanted to see her one last time.

With his wound enlarging and his skin decaying, Mark carries on killing. He gets sicker and sicker, he becomes weak and his leg breaks. He uses an electric screwdriver to fix a metal pole to his leg but he can't face looking in the mirror anymore because his face has become distorted. He decides enough is enough and takes an overdose of chloroform.

J IS FOR...

JUNK (2000)

Junk is a low-budget Japanese zombie movie. It was written and directed by Atsushi Muroga and stars Nobuyuki Asano in the lead role.

The story follows a gang of jewellery thieves who plan to meet up with the local Yakuza (mobsters) in an abandoned warehouse to sell their stolen goods. What they don't realise is that the warehouse was previously used by the US military as a place where scientists performed experiments on resurrecting the dead. The scientists used a formula called DNX (reanimation fluid) to resurrect the naked bodies of Japanese women. The formula worked in bringing the women back to life but had the side effect of turning them into zombies, hungry for human flesh. The scientists left the corpses locked in the warehouse, with the remainder of the DNX formula, while they tried to decide what to do.

When the thieves arrive at the warehouse to sell their goods, one of them is attacked by a zombie. The others are terrified and want to get out while they can, but as they do, the Yakuza arrive. The gangsters don't believe that a zombie attacked them and want the jewels they came for, without handing over any cash. They get into a gunfight with the thieves, who take shelter in a room full of corpses and DNX. In the continuing gunfight the liquid explodes over the corpses, bringing the dead back to life. Controlled by the first dead woman subjected to the Americans' experiment, the corpses attack – zombie madness and gunfights follow.

K IS FOR...

KING OF THE ZOMBIES (1941)

A classic zombie movie, *King of the Zombies* was directed by Jean Yarbrough. The movie was set during the Second World War, a theme that is apparent throughout, with an Austrian villain, German radio conversations and references to spies, although neither Germany nor Nazis are actually mentioned.

The movie starts when a small plane gets into trouble somewhere over the Caribbean. Blown off course and low on fuel, it is guided by a faint radio signal to an island, where it crash lands. The plane is carrying the pilot, James 'Mac' McCarthy, Bill Summers and his servant Jeff Jackson. Their mission was to find Admiral Arthur Wainwright, who went missing in the area.

The three men are given refuge on the island by the mysterious Dr Mikhail Sangre in his mansion. Jeff is immediately on edge about the Austrian doctor and his home, and quickly finds out that all is not as it seems. When Jeff is told to stay in the kitchen with another servant, he finds out that the help is not human. The mysterious doctor has zombies helping out at the mansion. Jeff tells the others of his discovery, and initially they don't believe his suspicions. Still, when he's attacked by the zombies, the others allow him to rest upstairs, where the strange goings-on continue.

That night, Jeff discovers that Dr Sangre's wife has been in the room via a secret door. Again he tells the others what he has seen. At first they don't believe him, but when he shows them an earring she dropped they realise he's been telling the truth. The three guests decide to go investigating downstairs, where Bill is attacked by a zombie. James also makes a discovery, finding the niece of the strange doctor in the mansion's library, looking at a book on hypnosis.

The following day, when James and Bill return to the crash site to use the radio on the plane, they discover the plane is missing. They decide to split up: Bill goes to find the doctor's radio, while James heads off to talk to the doctor's niece in the mansion. Later Bill discovers that both James and Jeff are missing.

Jeff has been hypnotised into thinking he's a zombie for a short time. When he manages to break the hypnosis, he meets up with James in the bedroom through the secret entrance. After they re-enter the secret door they come across a voodoo ritual in the cellar. The mad doctor discovers them and starts to attack them. The pair manage to fight him off and kill the Austrian.

It is revealed that the mysterious doctor was working for the Germans, attempting to gather information on the admiral the others were searching for. Through his mad experiments, he was trying to transfer the admiral's thoughts into his niece, so she could tell him everything he needed to know.

DID YOU KNOW?

This American film was released before the USA entered the Second World War. Two years after its release, a sequel followed, call *Revenge of the Zombies*.

L IS FOR...

LAND OF THE DEAD (2005)

Released by Universal Pictures, George A Romero's *Land of the Dead* was the fourth movie in the series and had the biggest budget of the Dead series to date. It received rave reviews and was a box office hit.

The movie shows an America devastated by a zombie epidemic that has spread across the whole country. Millions of people have died and have reanimated into cannibalistic zombies. Years have passed since the first outbreak and only a few small groups of humans are left. Many survivors have found refuge in Pennsylvania where the government and authorities have managed to gain control of a city. Three sides of the city are secured by rivers and the fourth is fenced off with electric cable to keep the zombies out. The city has its good and bad areas, with hilltop Fiddler's Green being the location of choice for the rich and powerful seeking to remain in the lap of luxury while the poor people live in squalor.

The city is also protected by an outstanding piece of engineering, a vehicle named Dead Reckoning. The vehicle is packed with ammunition, heavy-duty machine guns and video surveillance. It is fully equipped to take on any zombie attackers. The owner and manager of Fiddler's Green, Kaufman (Dennis Hopper) financed the construction of this great machine, with initial plans for it to be used as a sturdy launch base for fireworks. It has been discovered that zombies are fascinated by fireworks and will stop and stare in amazement. A firework display thus makes it easier for the humans to get about and to pick off zombies.

The chief designer and commander of Dead Reckoning is the newly retired Riley Denbo (Simon Baker). Riley has gained much respect over the years for protecting the city from danger and for bringing in much-needed food and medical supplies. When Riley visits a club owned by a man named Chihuahua, he discovers that the man is using a poor woman named Slack (Asia Argento) as bait to get two hungry zombies to fight as entertainment for his customers. This angers Riley and he decides to help her. With the help of his friend Charlie he saves Slack from near-death and kills Chihuahua in the process.

Later the trio are arrested and thrown in jail, and the men find out how Slack ended up in Chihuahua's live show. Slack reveals that she works for a man called Mulligan, a former colleague of Riley's who has been trying to get the poor people in the city to revolt against the current corrupt system. Kaufman had found this out and had ordered Chihuahua to have her killed.

While this is going on, Dead Reckoning's second in command Cholo DeMora (John Leguizamo) is told he will not get the apartment he was promised in Fiddler's Green. Cholo does not take no for an answer and after threatening to abolish Fiddler's Green altogether he gathers his troops: Pretty Boy, Mouse, Anchor and Foxy. The group capture Dead Reckoning and set out on their mission to hold Fiddler's Green to ransom. While they are doing this, zombies attack but Cholo doesn't care and tells his crew just to ignore them.

Kaufman is angry that Cholo has hijacked the city's defence vehicle and wants him stopped. He knows the only man who can do this is Riley. He gives Riley three of his own men to help him – Manolete, Pillsbury and Motown. Riley decides to take Charlie, Pillsbury and Slack on his mission, but refuses to take Motown because he thinks she has ulterior motives and wants to stop him. Once they set out, Slack has to kill Manolete when she discovers he has been bitten by a zombie. She knows they can't afford him to come back as a zombie.

When the group eventually locate Cholo, they exchange gunfire and Riley nearly dies. Motown turns up but is bitten by a zombie. Eventually Ridley gains control of Dead Reckoning by shutting its weaponry systems down. Riley negotiates with Cholo and agrees to take Dead Reckoning and head north, while Cholo takes an old battered station wagon and drives west, but he is attacked by a zombie on the way. Once bitten, Cholo turns back to the city in search of Kaufman. He wants to kill him before he turns into a zombie.

The zombies seem to be changing and growing in intelligence. A zombie nicknamed Big Daddy, who runs a petrol station and is not affected by fireworks, has been helping other zombies communicate through grunting and moaning, and teaching them how to use weapons and get into the city. They have learned how to avoid the water and wires, and start getting ready to attack the city.

Big Daddy finds Kaufman and follows him to a garage. He sees a car parked next to a petrol pump and comes up with a plan. He pours petrol through the car's broken windscreen. The zombified Cholo arrives and attacks Kaufman by biting him. While the two fight inside the garage, Big Daddy finds a propane tank, sets it alight and rolls it towards the car. The vehicle explodes, burning both Kaufman and Cholo to a crisp.

While the zombies are causing explosions, Riley returns to the city to save the remaining citizens with the aid of Dead Reckoning. All the once rich are now walking with the poor as undead zombies – class has no bearing when you're a zombie – but Riley's group find a few survivors who hid with Mulligan. They want to rebuild the city but Riley wants to leave. As they depart, Pretty Boy sees Big Daddy and his zombie group, who are also heading out of the city, and gets ready to kill them because they are in clear range but Riley stops her, telling her they are just looking for a place to go too. Riley and his crew then head for Canada in Dead Reckoning, firing fireworks as they go.

DID YOU KNOW?

The film was originally supposed to be handled by 20th Century Fox, but a dispute broke out over the movie's name. George's original plan was to name it *Dead Reckoning* but the studio, who wanted the rights to the Dead series, wanted to call it *Night of the Living Dead: Dead Reckoning*. George refused and went elsewhere.

DAN OLIVER

MOVIE MISTAKES

When the man is bitten on the wrist by the zombie at the start of the movie and shoots himself, the blood gushes from his head before he actually pulls the trigger.

During the scene in Chihuahua's club, one of the zombies gets red paint sprayed on his mouth but in the shot that follows the paint has disappeared.

When Kaufman shoots Big Daddy in the right shoulder he leaves bullet holes, but at the end of the movie Big Daddy has no bullet holes in his overalls.

M IS FOR...

MARK OF THE ASTRO-ZOMBIES (2002)

Directed and written by Ted V Mikels, *Mark of the Astro-Zombies* is based on his original *Astro-Zombies* movie, which was released in 1968. Released straight to video, this features Tura Satana as Malvira, Liz Renay as Crystal, Brinke Stevens as Cindy and Sean Morelli as Jeff.

In this reinterpretation of *Astro-Zombies*, the evil aliens are now performing surgery on humans, placing computer chips inside their brains and substituting their organs with synthetic ones. The Astro-Zombies have one thing in their sights – to kill all humans.

A pair of ruthless criminals read in the newspaper that people are being killed and that it looks like history is repeating itself as something similar has happened before. They decide they need to come up with a plan and start scheming about how they can capitalise on what the aliens are doing. They arrange a gathering of foreign representatives in order to deceive and trick them into paying billions of dollars for the power to control their own army of the walking dead.

Meanwhile, in the office of the President of the United States, a group of scholars meet to try to uncover the truth. Elsewhere, an FBI agent and a newspaper reporter are carrying out their own investigation to find out whether there really are aliens attacking people or whether it's a huge hoax.

MORTUARY (2005)

Directed by Tobe Hooper, *Mortuary* follows the Doyles – a widowed mortician and her two children – as they move to a small town in California to start a new life by re-opening an old funeral home. The abandoned house has a reputation with residents of the town, who believe it was built on a haunted site... Zombie madness follows!

The dream of starting a new life goes off-plan from

the outset. The widow, Leslie (Denise Crosby), quickly realises she has been duped by the guy selling the Fowler Brothers Funeral Home. It's in a much worse state than she had anticipated, has a septic sewer that needs attention, and there's a strange black fungus everywhere. Added to this, her teenage son Jonathan (Dan Byrd) hears about the legend of Bobby Fowler from Cal, Tina and Sara, whom he meets at the local diner. He also meets Liz, a girl he is attracted to and Grady her gay best friend.

The story goes that Bobby, a deformed and abused boy of the Fowler family, lived in the mortuary. Bobby mysteriously disappeared at the age of eight, but ten years later his parents were found murdered. Some locals believe Bobby Fowler is still alive. That night Cal, Tina and Sara decide to pay a visit to the graveyard outside the mortuary. They start vandalising the place, even going into one of the crypts, where they get a huge shock when they're attacked by Bobby (Price Carson).

The following day the local sheriff turns up at the mortuary to welcome Leslie and her family to the town. Jonathan and Liz have just been given some drugs by Grady. During the sheriff's visit he mentions that he's trying to stop 'graveyard babies' (teenagers who get pregnant after hooking up at the cemetery), and says that he's looking for the three who went missing in the graveyard the previous night. When he goes to investigate their disappearance, he also is attacked and infected by Bobby Fowler.

A day later, we see the other victims of Bobby Fowler. Cal and Sara turn up at the diner looking terrible. Things get worse for the pair as Cal has an attack of rage and Sara begins throwing up weird black ooze. Rita, who works at the diner, tries to help them out but is infected in the process – widening the impact of the original attack.

Back at the mortuary, things also take a turn for the worse. When Leslie is carrying out her first embalming, one of the dead bodies rises up, attacks her and infects her. She then tries to infect her son and his friends by preparing a soup from the gloopy black ooze seen earlier. In a stroke of good luck, one of Jonathan's friends, Liz, pours some salt into the soup, causing an unusual bubbling reaction. They know something is wrong, and Leslie starts to attack the group. Jonathan fights off his zombified mother and the four manage to escape.

Chased by another infected person, the group are forced to find refuge in a crypt in the graveyard. They find out that Bobby Fowler has been living in this crypt, and has constructed underground tunnels below the cemetery. Again Leslie attacks the group. They escape up a ladder that leads back to the house, where they barricade themselves in.

They start questioning Tina, who had escaped on the

night of the visit to the graveyard; they're not sure whether they can trust that she's not infected. To prove she's OK her hand is cut and shows it has blood, not black ooze, inside. But when she goes to the kitchen to clean the wound, black ooze has mixed with the water and infects her. This is shown when one of the group spills salt on her and burns her. Meanwhile, outside the house the sheriff, also infected, is spraying the house with shotgun fire.

With no options left and nowhere to hide, the group decide they've only got one choice – to fight. They go back down into the tunnels below the house, leaving Jonathan's sister Jamie behind as it's too dangerous. The three move around the tunnel, searching for the infected. Grady is the next one of the group to become a victim, when a hand punches him right through the chest. In his last breath he tells the other two to run, and they manage to escape.

The two manage to locate the source of the contagious black ooze – a well filled with it! While this is going on, Jamie, who was left at the house, is captured by Bobby Fowler and taken to his hideout. The three join together to confront the crazed zombie, throwing salt all over him. It works and Bobby is sucked in, giving them the chance to escape the tunnels. They manage to get as far as the house, but when they try to leave Jonathan is pulled underground by one of the infected, and Jamie is pulled back into the house by Leslie. The film ends leaving only the fate of Liz from the group open.

DID YOU KNOW?

The quote carved into the door on the crypt – 'That which is dead... Cannot eternal lie... With strange eons... Even death may die' – is from HP Lovecraft's short story 'The Call of Cthulhu'.

IS FOR...

NIGHT OF THE LIVING DEAD (1968)

The first movie in director George A Romero's Dead series, *Night of the Living Dead* is one of the best zombie movies ever and had a huge influence on the zombie horror genre. A black-and-white movie, it was written by George and John A Russo and produced by Karl Hardman and Russell Streiner. Russell also played the character of Johnny in the movie.

At the start of the movie Johnny and his sister Barbra (Judith O'Dea) are on their way to visit their father's grave. As they drive through the countryside Johnny teases Barbra about her fear of the graveyard, saying the famous words 'They are coming to get you, Barbra' and 'They are coming for you, Barbra.' As they make their way on foot they are approached by a man who is limping. Johnny jokes to his sister that the man is 'one of them' and Barbra feels that she must apologise for her brother.

As she gets closer to the man he grabs her and Johnny leaps to Barbra's defence. He struggles with the man but is knocked to the ground, hitting his head on the edge of a gravestone, which kills him. The pale-faced man turns his attention back to Barbra and she rushes to the car. She can't start the engine because the key is in Johnny's pocket, so she removes the handbrake. The car rolls down the hill, only to collide with a tree. Barbra has no choice but to leave the car and run for a farmhouse close by.

The man is still chasing her when she reaches the farmhouse, which is deserted. The man is soon joined by a group of people who walk just like him, as if they are in a trance. Barbra searches inside the house for someone to help her but to her horror she stumbles across a corpse that has been partly eaten. Barbra panics and tries to get out of the farmhouse but she is stopped by a man called Ben (Duane Jones) who arrives in a truck. He attacks the strange figures, takes her back inside and together they board up the doors and windows with whatever they can find.

While working they awkwardly exchange stories.

Ben is a drifter and describes the violence he has seen. Barbra becomes hysterical because she left her brother and she wants to know if he is OK. She hits Ben but he knocks her back with a blow to the face. Barbra is so hysterical that she passes out in shock on the sofa. As Barbra lies there Ben manages to get a rifle and a radio. By listening to the news on the radio, he learns that unpredictable outbursts of violence are spreading across the East Coast of the United States. The violent people seem to be in some sort of trance.

Barbra is startled as the cellar door swings open and a family emerge from their hiding place. Together they have to come up with a way of stopping their ghoul attackers. The older man, Harry (Karl Hardman), thinks it will be best to stay in the cellar but Ben says it is a death trap and they are better off upstairs. The younger man, Tom, agrees and tells his girlfriend Judy to come up from the cellar. Harry goes back to the cellar to find Helen (Marilyn Eastman) and his daughter Karen, who has been hurt and is very ill.

The news on the radio says the violent people are recently deceased human beings who have come back to life and want to feed on human flesh. The group turn on a television and learn more. They find out that specialist scientists and military generals are not certain what has caused this to happen, but one scientist is adamant that it is radiation emanating from a space probe that exploded in the Earth's atmosphere. The group also learn that the nearby town of Willard has a rescue station for humans to hide in, so the group plan how they can get there. They want to get medical assistance for Karen.

For their escape attempt the group need fuel for their truck, so Ben and Tom drive it to the gas pump while Harry throws Molotov cocktails at the ghouls. Judy wants to make sure that Tom is OK so she goes to him. In the rush, Tom spills some fuel and the truck is soon on fire. He jumps inside with Judy so they can move it a safe distance from the pump but it explodes and kills them. Their bodies are then devoured by the ghouls.

Ben gets back to the house but Harry has shut the door so he can't get in, making him an easy target for the ghouls. Ben is so angry that he kicks the door down and goes for Harry. While they are fighting the newsreaders assure listeners that a gunshot or heavy blow to the head will stop the ghouls and that there are armed people out in the countryside trying to halt them.

Harry threatens to kill Ben with his own rifle just as the ghouls attack. Ben manages to get the rifle off him and shoots him. The ghouls grab Helen and Barbra through the window and a dying Harry just makes it to the cellar to discover that Karen is dead. Helen manages to loosen the ghouls' grasp and goes to the cellar, where she sees Karen is no longer human and is eating Harry's corpse. Before she can retreat, Karen stabs her with a trowel.

Barbra is taken by a group of ghouls, leaving Ben as the last person alive. He locks himself in the cellar and shoots the undead Helen and Harry. He manages to fall asleep but wakes up when armed men arrive to sort out the ghouls. They bombard the farmhouse, killing any remaining zombies but when Ben emerges from the cellar they mistake him for a ghoul and shoot him. His body is burned alongside the rest.

DID YOU KNOW?

When *Night of the Living Dead* was first released it was heavily criticised for its unambiguous content and similarities to the Vietnam War taking place at the time.

Although the word 'zombie' is never used in the movie, George introduced cannibal zombies, who were dead people reanimated.

MOVIE MISTAKES

When Ben finds some shoes and a gun in the cupboard, he puts the shoes on Barbra but in the next shot she's not wearing any.

The corpse that Barbra finds when she first gets to the

farmhouse is missing part of its face, but when Ben moves it its face isn't damaged.

The zombies smash the headlights on Ben's truck but when Ben and Tom go to drive it to the gas pump the lights aren't broken.

NIGHT OF THE LIVING DEAD 3D (2006)

Night of the Living Dead 3D is a modern tribute to the 1968 movie. It was directed by Jeff Broadstreet, who is best known for directing the 2005 movie *Nightmare Hostel*. At the time of writing, he was working on *Night of the Living Dead 3D: Re-Animation*, due out in 2012.

Siblings Barb (Brianna Brown) and Johnny travel to the countryside for the funeral of their aunt. They arrive late so they drive straight to the cemetery. The graveyard is empty with no sign of the procession and suddenly they are attacked by zombies. Johnny escapes in his car, leaving Barb in the cemetery. Drug dealer and college student Ben (Joshua DesRoches) finds her and comes to her rescue, taking her on his motorbike to the security of the Cooper farmhouse. There they are joined by Henry (Greg Travis) and Hellie Cooper, their daughter Karen, farmhands Owen and Tom, and Tom's girlfriend Judy.

The farmhouse soon comes under attack from the flesh-eating zombies, who kill Tom and Judy in the barn. A local mortician called Gerald Tovar Jr (Sid Haig) arrives and tells them a creepy tale about where the zombies originally came from.

Owen and Karen are the next to die and they become zombies. Henry and Hellie decide to lock themselves upstairs in the farmhouse but Henry has been bitten and will soon die. They both decide to commit suicide before this happens. Ben and Barb decide that the best thing to do is leave with Gerald, but this proves to be a big mistake.

Gerald takes them to his house but knocks Ben unconscious. He then explains to Barb that he was the one who created the zombies as he wanted his dead father to live again. He fed his dad his own blood to satisfy his thirst. Barb is shocked and sets the house alight, but before she can escape Gerald takes her and the unconscious Ben hostage in his mortuary.

Gerald's plan is to have Barb killed by the zombies so that she becomes one, but she manages to stop him and he ends up being eaten. Ben has come around by this point and quickly leaves with Barb. They lock the zombies in the garage so they can't come after them but then Ben notices that he has been impaled with a tyre iron, and in matter of moments he turns into a zombie. Barb has only one bullet left in her gun so she kills him quickly. As she shoots, the zombies break out and she gives up, knowing there is no point in fighting the inevitable. She screams and the credits roll.

O IS FOR...

ONE DARK NIGHT (1983)

Also known as *Entity Force* (its UK video title), *One Dark Night* was directed by Tom McLoughlin. It was nominated for Best Horror Film of 1983 by the Academy of Science Fiction, and stars Robin Evans as Carol, Leslie Speights as Kitty and Meg Tilly as Julie.

The movie follows a new girl in town, led into an initiation ceremony to try to make some friends. But what the group, known as The Sisters, don't realise is that the crypt used in the initiation ceremony is haunted by an evil ghost, intent on killing. The ghost is the spirit of a Russian occultist called Karl 'Raymar'

Rhamarevich. Before his death, this odd man found a way of becoming powerful once he had died, through the power of telekinesis.

When Raymar died, his body was found in strange circumstances. Six girls had been murdered in his apartment, all stuffed into a closet, and plates and other objects were stuck in the walls. When Raymar's body was removed from the apartment, bolts of electricity flew out of the fingers of his corpse.

Raymar's daughter Olivia wasn't on speaking terms with her father, but after the circumstances of his death are explained to her and her husband Allan, they find out from Samuel Dockstader, a writer for *The World of the Occult* and a former friend of Raymar, that he had powers far beyond a normal man. The writer tells the pair that the deceased was actually a psychic vampire who got powers of telekinesis by kidnapping young girls, scaring them and then feeding off their bioenergy.

The Sisters know nothing about Raymar's death, and when Carol, Kitty and Leslie drop the new girl Julie at the crypt, they don't realise that Raymar's body has been buried there only that afternoon. The snobby girls have arranged the initiation as revenge, as Julie's new boyfriend Steve was previously going out with Carol. To make her night worse, they give her a flashlight with no batteries and tablets to keep her awake. Julie enters the crypt and takes a look around. All seems OK, and she gets ready to bed in for the night, laying her bag down on the floor. At this point, unbeknown to Julie, cracks start to appear around the vault and the terror begins!

Meanwhile, Carol and Kitty have planned some horror of their own to make Julie's night as bad as possible. They sneak into the crypt, bringing with them scary masks and fake blood. They start their plan to scare Julie, throwing a vase on the floor to wake her up, smearing the fake blood everywhere, planting a fake severed hand, and dressing up as a ghost. It all works and the terrified Julie retreats under a pew and prays for her life.

Pleased with their efforts, the pair celebrate with a joint of cannabis under the vault of Raymar. The horror they brought on Julie is nothing compared with what they go through, as suddenly the walls of the crypt start to shake violently, and with windows smashing and furniture flying around the room, it's clear that this is no prank. Then Raymar's vault opens to reveal a hellish red glow inside. As the girls try to escape, the vaults start opening, and the dead begin to rise out of them. The girls find themselves overpowered by a gang of zombies and there is nothing they can do.

When Julie's boyfriend, Steve, finds out about the initiation plan from the other 'sister', Leslie, he quickly makes his way to the crypt. Meanwhile, Raymar's estranged daughter Olivia has found out about the powers her father had gained before his death, and also heads there.

Steve arrives at the crypt unaware of Raymar and his powers. He convinces Julie that it's all a prank, but when zombies start closing in on the couple they realise that something else is going on. Steve tries to put up a fight but the zombies overpower him. Olivia arrives and tries using the same powers as her father to destroy him. His powers are too strong for her, but in a last ditch attempt she uses a mirror to reflect the lightning bolts he's shooting at her back onto him. This works, and Raymar is turned to dust along with the zombies.

DID YOU KNOW?

The editing of the film was carried out without the contribution or consent of its director Tom McLoughlin. When the director saw the final version and found that the ending had been cut, he managed to convince the producers to shoot a final scene. This was shot in Tom's garage, with the actors and crew working for free!

P IS FOR...

PEGG, SIMON

Actor, writer, producer, director and all-round funny man, Simon Pegg made his impact on the zombie scene with his critically acclaimed movie *Shaun of the Dead*.

Simon graduated from Bristol University in 1991 with a degree in film, theatre and television. His professional career started gathering motion in 1993 when he moved to London and joined the stand-up comedy circuit. Two years later he was invited to the Edinburgh Festival, which has been a springboard for many comedy careers. Following his show there, he was asked to appear at festivals in Australia, where he gained more attention.

After several TV and radio appearances, Simon's big break came with the Channel 4 sitcom *Spaced*, which he co-wrote with Jessica Stevenson. This brought him a nomination for Best Male Comedy Newcomer at the British Comedy Awards.

His next big project was the zombie comedy movie *Shaun of the Dead*. Following great reaction from critics and film fans, Simon was invited to make an appearance in infamous zombie director George A Romero's *Land of the Dead* movie. A zombie fan, Simon also appeared as a zombie hunter in *Danger! 50,000 Zombies!* – a British spoof documentary short featuring Nick Frost.

The next instalment in what Simon calls his Blood and Ice Cream trilogy was *Hot Fuzz*. Another comedy with paranormal undertones, the movie follows Simon and Nick Frost as policemen in a rural village. It is reported that the final film of the trilogy has been planned, to be named *The World Ends*.

Simon's other film credits include the alien comedy *Paul* (again alongside Nick Frost), and another *Star Trek* movie scheduled for 2012, where he again plays the iconic Montgomery 'Scotty' Scott.

DID YOU KNOW?

Pegg has named the paranormal TV series *The X-Files* as one of his favourite shows.

PET SEMATARY (1989)

Pet Sematary is a horror movie based on the novel of the same name by Stephen King. It was directed by Mary Lambert, who had made her name with pop videos for Madonna ('Borderline', 'Like a Virgin', 'Material Girl') and Janet Jackson ('Nasty', 'Control'). Mary had made her debut as a movie director in 1987 with the controversial thriller *Siesta*, starring Ellen Barkin and Jodie Foster.

At the start of the movie the Creed family are upping sticks from Chicago and moving to a house near the small town of Ludlow in Maine, USA. The family consists of parents Louis (Dale Midkiff) and Rachel (Denise Crosby) and their young children Ellie (Blaze Berdahl) and Gage (Miko Hughes). They also have a cat called Winston Churchill or Church for short. Their new home is situated next to a busy highway, and the family are warned by their new neighbour Jud Crandall (Fred Gwynne) that the road is notorious for high-speed truck drivers from the local chemical plant.

Louis and Jud become friends and after a few weeks they go on a walk in the woods behind their homes. The woods lead to the local pet cemetery, which is spelt 'sematary' on the sign. The children in the local town bury their pets here after they have been killed on the highway.

Louis works as a doctor at the local university hospital. After treating a victim of a fatal car accident, he experiences something really strange that night. The victim, Victor Pascow, comes to visit him as a corpse. At first Louis thinks it is a dream. Victor walks Louis through the cemetery and warns him of the burial ground supposedly at the back of it, cautioning him not to go past the 'deadfall' (a mound of trees and bushes) at the back. Louis wakes up confused to find his feet covered in dirt. He assumes he must have been sleepwalking.

On Halloween, Jud's wife Norma nearly dies from a fatal heart attack but Louis manages to save her life. Rachel and the kids are back in Chicago but their cat Church gets run over on the busy highway. Jud wishes to repay Louis for all his help with Norma and decides to take Louis to the pet sematary to give Church a proper burial. However, Jud leads Louis to the cemetery beyond the deadfall, supposedly an ancient burial ground for a Native American tribe called the Micmacs. This is the burial ground that Victor warned him about. Jud tells Louis to bury Church next to a memorial sign.

The following day Church returns home reincarnated, acting in an unusual manner – almost as if he is 'a little dead', as Louis says. The cat gives off an unpleasant scent and instead of eating his prey he violently shreds it.

Several months later Gage is tragically run over by a speeding truck while out on a family picnic. Still grieving, Louis decides to bury Gage in the Native American burial ground beyond the deadfall in the hope that he will come back to life like Church did. Jud tries to stop him by recounting what happened to Timmy Baterman, a Second World War casualty who was buried there, only to come back to terrify the people of the town. Jud and his friends had to stop him so they set the house on fire to kill him but his father was killed as well.

Louis's wife decides to take Ellie to Chicago but she doesn't want to go because Victor has visited her in a dream. She knows her dad is about to do something dangerous and wants him to come with them instead. He refuses and once they have gone he goes to take Gage's body to the human cemetery. He sees Victor, who warns him not to cross the barrier, but he ignores the warning.

Ellie has another nightmare and tells her mother what happened. Rachel starts to believe what her daughter is saying. She rings Louis but gets no answer so she rings Jud. She tells him they are coming back but

Jud warns her not to. Victor's spirit tries one last time to stop Louis but he fails and Gage's body is buried.

It doesn't take long for the undead Gage to reappear. He enters the house, takes a scalpel from his father's case and heads to Jud's house for a game of hide and seek. He murders Jud by slicing his Achilles tendon, slashing his mouth and ripping his throat out.

Later that day Rachel returns home after worrying about Ellie's nightmare, and to her disbelief she finds Gage dressed in one of Jud's old hats. He shows her the scalpel but, ignoring it, she hugs her son in utter shock that he is alive. Unfortunately for her, Gage stabs his mother with the scalpel through her eyeball.

Louis has been asleep all this time and when he wakes up he sees his son's muddy footprints on the floor. He notices his scalpel is missing and then receives a mysterious call from Gage. His undead son says: 'Come play with me, Daddy! First I played with Jud, and then I played with Mommy. We had an awful good time. Now I want to play with you.'

Louis prepares lethal shots of morphine, testing them on Church, and the cat dies instantly. Searching Jud's house, Louis find his wife's corpse as she hangs from the attic by her neck. Suddenly Gage jumps out and attacks his father, biting and stabbing him. Louis manages to hold him off and injects him with morphine. An upset Gage walks away saying 'No fair!' before he dies.

Seeing his wife dead and his son undead turns Louis

mentally ill. He burns down Jud's house and carries his wife's body to the burial ground, saying he waited too long with Gage but Rachel will come back as her true self if he buries her quickly. The movie ends with Louis playing solitaire, and an undead Rachel calls out to him. As she says 'darling', her mouth sounds as if it is full of soil.

DID YOU KNOW?

Stephen King got the idea for *Pet Sematary* when his daughter's cat was killed on the busy highway outside his home.

Originally George A Romero was hired as director but he dropped out when filming was delayed.

Bruce Campbell was the first choice for the role of Louis but the part ended up going to Dale Midkiff.

A sequel called *Pet Sematary Two* came out in 1992. It was also directed by Mary Lambert, but it wasn't as popular as the first movie.

THE PLAGUE (2006)

The Plague is a horror movie directed and written by Hal Masonberg, who had previously only directed a short called *Mrs Greer. Dawson's Creek* actor James Van Der Beek stars as Tom, with Ivana Miličevi as Jean and Brad Hunt as Sam. The zombies in the movie are all children.

The story starts by explaining that one day all the children in the world under the age of nine contracted a disease that put them into a catatonic state. From then on, every child born fell into the catatonic state. The children gained super-strength and had fits twice a day but no explanation could be found. They were kept in hospitals and in disused schools, lined up in beds with doctors looking after them.

Ten years later, they all wake up at the same time and attack the people who have been caring for them. They want to kill all adults and set about doing just that. The children are super-clever and are mentally linked to each other, so that when one learns something they all learn it simultaneously. They learn how to use guns and damage the engines in the town's cars so the adults can't escape them easily. For every person they kill they take their soul.

Tom has recently been released from prison and has just moved in with his brother Sam. His nephew is one of the children in a catatonic state. Tom was married but his ex-wife Jean doesn't want anything to do with him anymore. Tom still loves her and when the children wake up and start attacking adults, Tom and Jean reunite and lead a group of adults in the hope that they can make it to a base 60km away.

PLANET TERROR (2007)

An American action horror film set in Texas, *Planet Terror* was directed and scripted by Robert Rodriguez, who is most famous for directing *Sin City* and *Once Upon a Time in Mexico*. Robert co-produced *Planet Terror* with Quentin Tarantino and Elizabeth Avellan.

The movie starts with a go-go dancer called Cherry Darling (Rose McGowan) quitting her job. She runs into her mechanic ex-boyfriend El Wray (Freddy Rodriguez) at the Bone Shack, a BBQ restaurant. Close by, military officials are taking part in a highly dangerous business transaction involving deadly quantities of a biochemical agent called DC2. The code name for this transaction is Project Terror. The man behind DC2 is a chemical engineer called Abby and the military officials are led by Lieutenant Muldoon (Bruce Willis).

Muldoon finds out that Abby has an extra supply of DC2 and attempts to hold him hostage. Abby releases the deadly gas into the air and it reaches the local

DAN OLIVER

towns. The residents who come into contact with it turn into bloodthirsty crazies. The people who are not infected give them the nickname the 'sickos' because they are capable of anything.

Dr William Block (Josh Brolin) and his anaesthesiologist wife Dakota (Marley Shelton) are in charge of treating the sickos in the local hospital. Unknown to her husband, Dakota is bisexual and has been cheating on him with a woman called Tammy. Meanwhile Cherry Darling and El Wray have hit the road in his truck but experience zombie attacks along the way, causing him to crash, after which several sicko zombies grab Cherry Darling and tear off her right leg. El Wray rushes her to the hospital.

Tammy, Dakota's former lover, is on her way to reunite with her when she too is attacked by the sickos. When her body is taken to the hospital, Dr Block realises who Tammy is when he sees her corpse and reads a text message from her phone. When he finds out she was the woman his wife was going to leave him for, he attacks his wife with her syringe, repeatedly stabbing her hand until she no longer moves. He locks her in a cupboard and carries on with his job attending to waiting patients, who are showing signs of the disease. Cherry Darling seems unaffected, even though she was bitten by one of the sickos.

Sheriff Hague arrives and decides to arrest El Wray over something he has done in the past but he escapes just in time to reach Cherry Darling at the hospital. The sickos are taking over and El Wray quickly straps a table leg to where her leg used to be. While all this is going on, Dakota flees to her car but breaks her wrist trying to open the car door with her numbed hand. Dr Block becomes infected by his zombie patients but El Wray and Cherry Darling manage to get out in time and head for the Bone Shack to hide.

Dakota goes to find her son Tony who suffers from autism and they head to her dad's house. He is a Texas Ranger and she thinks they will be safe there. Tony stupidly shoots himself in the face with the revolver his mother gives him, even after being told not to point it at himself.

When the scene changes, Sheriff Hague is shown shot in the neck by one of his officers, the Bone Shack is on fire and zombies are multiplying by the minute. Dakota, her dad and Tony's babysitters end up at the Bone Shack too. The group break out of the restaurant and head for the military base, but their way is blocked by a mass of zombies on a bridge. Muldoon and his men appear behind the zombies, kill them and arrest the surviving group.

When the group come across chemical engineer Abby, they find out that the military are infected too but have stolen Abby's dangerous gas because they can use it to delay them dying and turning into zombies. Muldoon has captured the group of survivors because they are immune to the gas, which means they may hold a solution to curing people who have been infected.

Soldiers (played by Quentin Tarantino and Greg Kelly, labelled as rapist 1 and 2) take Cherry Darling and Dakota away. The others escape from their cell in the base, although JT, the owner of the restaurant, gets shot. They find Muldoon and discover that he killed Osama Bin Laden before he and the rest of the soldiers became infected by DC2 and received orders to protect the area. El Wray then praises Muldoon and his troops for killing Osama Bin Laden and for their service to the area before killing Muldoon as he turns into a zombie.

While this is going on the rapist soldiers make Cherry Darling dance for them while pointing a gun at her, but she attacks one of them with her table leg and stabs him in the eye. Dakota, who has regained feeling in her hand, gets her syringe and attacks the second soldier with it. El Wray and Abby come to save Cherry Darling and Dakota at just the right time. El Wray fixes a modified M4 carbine with a M203 grenade launcher to where Cherry's leg used to be so she can use it to kill her rapist and several sickos as well.

After the group flee, the injured JT sets off explosives, killing himself and all the remaining sickos. The group decide to steal a helicopter so they can escape but encounter more sickos. Abby is killed by a flying missile that blows his head off, and El Wray is mortally wounded by a sicko soldier. The group decide to use the blades from the propeller to kill the rest of the sickos.

In the closing scene, Cherry Darling with her weapon of a leg takes charge, leading the group to a remote beach in Mexico, with many survivors joining them along the way. Cherry Darling gives birth to El Wray's daughter, which explains his sly comment earlier as he touches her belly and quotes his motto: 'I never miss.' The closing credits show Tony, Dakota's son, playing on the beach with his pet turtle, scorpion and tarantula.

DID YOU KNOW?

Robert came up with the idea for the movie while shooting his earlier hit *The Faculty* in 1998.

Q IS FOR...

QUARANTINE (2008)/QUARANTINE 2: TERMINAL (2011)

Although *Quarantine* is a shot-for-shot remake of the Spanish zombie film *[REC]* (2007), it is not quite identical. *REC* was set in Barcelona but *Quarantine* follows the same story – about a quarantined apartment block whose inhabitants show signs of a virus that turns them into bloodthirsty killers – in Los Angeles, with some added scenes and dialogue. It was directed by John Erick Dowdle.

Set for release in 2011, *Quarantine 2* picks up where the

first film left off. (Unlike its predecessor, *Quarantine 2* deviates from the plot of the Spanish original, *[REC]^2*.) This sequel starts later the same night at LAX airport, as passengers board a flight to Nashville. One of them starts showing the same strange symptoms seen by residents of the apartment block, forcing the aircraft to make an emergency landing. When the plane lands the flight crew and passengers realise they have been quarantined, and are trapped on board. The movie follows the plight of the newbie flight attendant Jenny, who plans to escape with a passenger.

R IS FOR...

RABID (1977)

A zombie horror movie, *Rabid* was written and directed by David Cronenberg, one of the first directors to create horror based on infections and body-alterations. He is best known for his movies *The Fly*, *A History of Violence*, *eXistenZ* and *Eastern Promises*.

The story starts with Rose (Marilyn Chambers) being admitted to a plastic surgery clinic in Montreal after a motorcycle accident leaves her close to death. Doctor Keloid (Howard Ryshpan) is given the task of trying to repair her broken body and save her life. He uses risky experimental surgery to give her skin grafts but her skin and organs are so damaged that it looks like she will die.

Rose is transformed – her skin and organs are working but she's now a zombie. She has a phallic stinger under her armpit that she uses to get blood from her victims and she wipes their memories so they have no recollection of what she has done to them. However, they can't continue with their normal lives because she infects them and they turn into zombies too. They each develop a lust for blood and set about biting people who come into contact with them.

The city is soon in chaos and martial law is declared, but Rose is in denial about being the carrier of the virus. Eventually she decides to see if the theory is true, but, after picking up a man and biting him, she is killed by the resulting zombie. Her body is thrown out with the garbage and with it goes probably any hope of finding a medical solution to the zombie madness…

The movie was given 61 out of a possible 100 by Rotten Tomatoes. *Time Out* magazine wrote in its review: 'As a maker of sci-fi/horror movies, Cronenberg seems obsessed with the links between sex and violence as well as the *Body Snatchers* theme of a possessed community. His earlier combination of the two strains in *Shivers* was too mechanically lurid and derivative to be very effective, but *Rabid* is far more successful. This time Cronenberg has opened up his story so that it literally portrays the panic and slow devastation of a whole Canadian city: a new strain of rabies reduces its victims to foaming murderous animals, and Cronenberg examines the mysterious sexual agency behind the plague with bewitching ambiguity.

'Rabid is also far better staged than its predecessor, and the best scenes, including one classic episode in a chicken takeaway, are pitched ingeniously between shock and parody, never quite succumbing to farce. None of the other recent apocalypse movies has shown so much political or cinematic sophistication.'

The reviewer from *Variety* summed up this movie when he wrote: '*Rabid*, as the dictionary explains, means both "affected with rabies" and "extremely violent". Using both definitions, *Rabid* is so accurately titled that this one word tells all. Here is an extremely violent, sometimes nauseating, picture about a young woman affected with rabies, running around Montreal infecting others.'

RE-ANIMATOR (1985)

Directed by Stuart Gordon, *Re-Animator* is the first movie in a series of three. Based on the HP Lovecraft story 'Herbert West – Reanimator', the blackly humorous movie has become a cult classic among horror and zombie fans around the world.

The story starts at a medical school in Zurich, Switzerland, where a policeman and a nurse are investigating strange noises coming from one of the labs. In the lab they find a student, Herbert West (Jeffrey Combs), attempting to bring the dead Professor Gruber back to life. The experiment fails and the professor's eyes explode from his head before he falls back to the floor.

We then follow Herbert to Miskatonic University in New England, where he plans to take his studies further. He rents a room from med student Dan Cain (Bruce Abbott), and sets about starting his experiments again. Without the use of a lab, Herbert converts the basement of his building and manages to get Dan on board with his idea of 'reanimation' – much to the displeasure of Dan's girlfriend Megan Halsey (Barbara Crampton), who doesn't trust Herbert after finding his 'reanimated' dead cat!

The pair are barred from the school after Dr Carl Hill (David Gale) has a run-in with Herbert, who accuses him of stealing the late Professor Gruber's work. This doesn't stop them, though, and they break into the morgue and start testing on human corpses. Their experiment goes wrong, and a corpse attacks the pair and then the head of the school, Dean Halsey, who stumbles across them. Herbert kills the zombie, and then injects the newly dead dean with the reagent.

Dr Hill finds out about the experiments and takes

the zombified Halsey into his custody. But it turns out that the students aren't the only ones performing mad experiments: Dr Hill has lobotomised Dean Halsey so he can control him, as he is obsessed with his daughter Megan.

Later, Dr Hill tries to blackmail Herbert and take credit for his work, but Herbert doesn't stand for it and chops off the doctor's head, turning both it and the separated body into zombies. Dr Hill's headless body fights back and knocks Herbert out, before carrying the head out of the office and ordering the zombie Halsey to kidnap Megan.

Herbert and Dan trace Halsey and Dr Hill back to the morgue, where they find Megan trapped. They free her, and she manages to command the zombie of her father to fight off the army of zombies Dr Hill has built. Her father's zombified body manages to kill the detached head of Dr Hill, but is then torn apart by the other zombies. In an attempt to kill the body of Dr Hill and hopefully bring this madness to an end, Herbert tries to give it an overdose of the reagent. But this doesn't work, and instead of destroying the headless zombie it causes it to mutate and attack Herbert.

As Dan and Megan flee, a zombie attacks Megan but Dan manages to get her body to the hospital. After failing to revive her, he decides to inject her with the reagent, and the film ends with her zombified screams...

DID YOU KNOW?

Originally, Gordon was going to adapt Lovecraft's story for the stage, but eventually decided, along with the writers, that a TV show was a better format. Plans changed again, however, when Gordon met producer Brian Yuzna, who convinced Gordon to shoot it as a movie in Hollywood because of all the special effects involved.

[REC] (2007)

[REC] is a Spanish horror movie, first released in its homeland. It was remade almost shot for shot the following year in the US and renamed *Quarantine*. The original was shot using shaky camerawork, similar to the hits *The Blair Witch Project* and *Cloverfield* and scenes in *District 9*. The clever use of the camera gives the audience a great idea of the fear, angst and tension the characters are feeling.

The movie starts with television reporter Ángela Vidal and her cameraman, Pablo, working an overnight shift at a Barcelona fire station while filming for a television series called *While You're Asleep*. The chaos kicks off when the fire station gets a call about an old woman trapped in her apartment. The journalists arrive to see the police kicking down the apartment door to find a crazed woman inside. The old woman is aggressive towards her would-be helpers, biting one of the policemen and then a fire fighter, causing him to fall down the stairwell to the ground floor.

While this is going on, the military and fire crews seal off the building, leaving Ángela and Pablo trapped inside, along with scared residents. In a tense scene, the pair decide to go back to the old woman's apartment, together with the remaining police officer and fire fighter. Again the old woman tries to attack them, leaving the police officer no choice but to shoot her.

Still trapped inside, the film crew start filming other residents, with a young girl Jennifer explaining that she and her dog have recently become ill. Although Jennifer's mother attributes her daughter's symptoms to tonsillitis, the audience knows something darker is lurking underneath…

Suspicions are confirmed when a health worker arrives at the block wearing a safety suit, in an attempt to treat injured residents. But despite their apparently serious injuries, the group turn on him. He explains that the apartment block has become infected by a disease whose symptoms take varying amounts of time to appear, depending on the person's blood type. He tells them that the previous day a dog taken from the block (Jennifer's dog Max) turned on other animals in the vet's surgery, attacking and killing them. The dog was then killed, but health workers had traced it back to this block.

On hearing this news, Jennifer turns to her mother and suddenly attacks her. The health worker explains to the terrified residents that the mystery virus they've been exposed to turns people into bloodthirsty savages.

As time progresses, so does the spread of the disease. More people in the apartment block become infected, leaving Ángela and Pablo to fight them off. The pair find out that there's a way out of the block through the sewer system, but they need to get to the fifth floor to get the key. Now the only human survivors left, they manage to locate the key, but, under attack from the bloodthirsty zombie residents, they're forced to head further up the building, rather than down towards the sewer escape route.

Once they reach the penthouse, they start to search. They find out that the apartment's former owner was an agent of the Vatican, who was researching a virus suspected of being a biological cause of demonic possession. The Vatican agent had found a young girl 'possessed' by this illness, kidnapped her and held her in the penthouse, in an attempt to research her case and find a cure. But while he was carrying out his research, the 'zombie virus' mutated to become contagious. The agent decided there was no hope for the girl, sealed her in the room to die, and left

Barcelona. Despite his attempts to seal the room, the disease had obviously spread.

Pablo discovers the entrance to the sealed room, and the pair see the scary figure of the girl left to die. Pablo tries to escape, but is caught by the infected girl and attacked horrifically. Ángela picks up Pablo's camera and runs, but trips and drops it. The audience then hears Ángela's screams as the dropped camera continues to roll, and she is dragged into the darkness.

Critics and horror fans loved the movie and it has an incredible score of 96 out of 100 on Rotten Tomatoes. Matthew Turner from the ViewLondon website wrote: 'Superbly acted, brilliantly directed and absolutely bloody terrifying, this is one of the best films of the year.'

Mark Salisbury of *Total Film* was equally impressed: 'Gripping, unsettling and truly horrific, *[REC]* is much more than the gimmick suggested by its title. Prepare to squirm, wince and wonder at how a potential *Blair Witch* knock-off is quite so grimy and engrossing. And don't eat dinner before you see it.'

DID YOU KNOW?

None of the actors who worked on [REC] were given full copies of the script. This meant they never knew the fate of their characters, adding to the tension of the whole movie. This was emphasised in the final scenes, which were shot in complete darkness using an infrared camera, leaving the actors clueless about what was going to jump out!

[REC]2 (2009)

Written and directed by the creators of its predecessor, Jaume Balagueró and Paco Plaza, $[REC]^2$ follows straight on from where the first movie ended.

The movie follows Dr Owen from the Spanish Ministry of Health and a Grupo Especial de Operaciones (GEO) team equipped with helmet-mounted video cameras, as they enter the locked-down apartment block in Barcelona. The GEO team is sent in to try to take control of the situation, while Owen (who's actually a priest) goes in to try to get a blood sample from the first infected person – the girl who attacked Ángela and Pablo at the end of the first film.

They all head for the penthouse, where the girl was

kept, only to find that the girl is nowhere to be seen. The air ducts of the building are being used by the infected to get from room to room. One of the GEO team enters the air duct and finds a sample of the girl's blood from the original tests the priest had carried out. Owen performs a religious ceremony on the blood, which is infected with a virus that is believed to demonically possess people. The blood suddenly bursts into flame, confirming it is that of the infected girl, but leaving Owen in need of another sample, forcing him to hunt for the girl.

Meanwhile, the father of another infected victim is outside the apartment block. His daughter Jennifer was the young girl who spoke to Ángela in the apartment block in the first film, explaining that she and her dog had become sick, before turning on her mother. Jennifer's father was out of the building getting medicine for his daughter when the quarantine started. He manages to convince a fireman to take him into the building.

Three uninfected teenagers also end up in the building, after playing about on the rooftops and then finding the entrance from the sewer. The police realise the gang have gained access and decide to seal their entrance to contain the infection. The three teenagers find Jennifer's father and the fireman who helped him get in. The group then find Ángela Vidal, whose fate in the first movie had seemed to be certain death. As the group move around the building, they're subjected to attacks from the residents.

One of the teenagers, Tito, becomes infected. The others manage to restrain him, forcing him to tell them the whereabouts of the girl; he says 'the highest', which they interpret as meaning the penthouse. Tito tells them that the light blinds them from seeing the path, and they realise that she can only be seen in the dark.

When the group reach the penthouse, they turn the camera's night vision on and enter the secret room, where they find the girl. After a struggle, Ángela shoots her, leaving Owen without the blood sample he came for. Ángela tells Owen to authorise their exit from the quarantined building, but, still needing a sample, he refuses to do so. Enraged, Ángela starts beating Owen to force him to let them out, and when Rosso, a member of the GEO team, tries to stop her she kills him. This is when they realise that Ángela is infected. She then kills Owen, takes his radio, and in his voice calls for the mission to be called off, and that there's one survivor: a woman called Ángela...

We then see the ending of the first movie again, from the point where Ángela was dragged into the darkness by the infected girl. We see the girl climbing on top of her and infecting her through her mouth.

> ### DID YOU KNOW?
>
> Many of the shrieks, screams and shouts you can hear in the film were added after filming. With so many scary scenes, the actors' dialogue would have been drowned out by all the screaming, so sound technicians added the effects in post-production.

RESIDENT EVIL (2002)

This big-budget zombie movie followed on from the popular Resident Evil console games by Capcom. It was directed by Paul WS Anderson and did well at the box office, grossing more than $100 million worldwide.

The movie starts inside a top-secret genetic research station called the Hive, which is owned by the Umbrella Corporation and located under Raccoon City. The underground facility has become infected by an outbreak of the mysterious T-virus, after a thief threw a vial of it into a lab full of workers. The facility's artificial intelligence control centre, called the Red Queen, detects the outbreak and locks down the Hive, sealing everyone inside.

Meanwhile Alice (Milla Jovovich) wakes up in an empty mansion, suffering from amnesia. Along with a police officer, Matt (Eric Mabius), and another amnesia sufferer called Spence, she is taken by a group of commandos working for the Umbrella Corporation and escorted to an underground station that leads to the Hive. The head of the commandos, One, explains that everyone in the group apart from Spence is an employee of the corporation, and that the amnesia was caused by a nerve gas released by the Hive's artificial intelligence system.

When the group attempt to shut down the artificial intelligence system at the Hive, several of them are killed by an automatic laser system. The remaining commandos manage to disable the Red Queen, despite the system's warnings. When the system shuts down it causes a power cut in the facility, disabling the automatic doors and releasing the swarm of staff who have turned into zombies. One of the commandos, Rain, becomes infected by the zombies while fighting.

When Matt and Alice are separated from the other survivors, Matt manages to locate his missing sister, Lisa, who has turned into a zombie too. Alice also makes a discovery, when a pack of experimental dogs attack her. She is able to fend the beasts off with a combination of martial arts. Alice then uses these skills to save Matt, who is being attacked by his sister.

The plot thickens as Alice's memories begin to come back to her. She remembers being Lisa's contact – the person Matt believes is responsible for his sister turning into a zombie. She keeps her lips sealed and they

 DAN OLIVER

reunite with the other survivors to try to escape through maintenance tunnels.

Alice also starts getting memories of an anti-virus that exists, but when they come across a lab, they find that both it and the original virus are missing. Spence's memory is also coming back, and he realises that he was the one who took the vials. He remembers he hid them on a train in the underground system, but before he can get to them he's killed by a mutated creature called a Licker. Rain is the next casualty, when Matt kills her as she's turned into a zombie.

Matt and Alice manage to make it back to the mansion but Matt starts mutating from an injury caused by the Licker. Before Alice can help, the pair are overpowered by Umbrella scientists. They tell Alice he's being taken away for the Nemesis program and then knock her out.

The movie ends with Alice waking up strapped to a table in the city hospital. She manages to escape and finds the hospital and Raccoon City deserted. Amid signs of chaos, she sees a newspaper clipping that reveals the T-virus spread to the city, creating an army of zombies.

DID YOU KNOW?

The filmmakers hired professional dancers to star as the zombies, as they had great control over their bodies.

MOVIE MISTAKES

When the Licker scratches Matt you can see the scratches appear on his arm before it even touches him.

Rain has her hair hanging down on the left side of her face when she is asked why a zombie is still standing after being shot five times, but in the next shot her hair is hanging down on both left and right-hand sides.

The papers around Lisa's dead zombie body move depending on the shot.

RESIDENT EVIL: AFTERLIFE 3D (2010)

In this fourth movie in the Resident Evil series, Alice continues her battle against the Umbrella Corporation as the T-virus spreads through the US, turning its victims into the undead. A lead suggesting a safe haven from the virus takes her to Los Angeles, only to find it swarming with zombies. She searches for and rescues survivors and they team up against Albert Wesker, the head of the Umbrella Corporation.

Alice's clones try to kill Wesker at his base in Tokyo, where the previous film (*Resident Evil: Extinction*) left off. After hearing emergency signals from an area in Alaska known to be safe for survivors, she takes a plane there. When she arrives there are no signs of life, until she finds Claire, holed up in the woods and subjected to an Umbrella mind control device that has wiped her memory.

Later the pair find more survivors, trapped in a prison surrounded by zombies. They fly in to help, and learn that the safe haven in Alaska known as Arcadia is actually a cargo tanker travelling along the coast. Now needing a route out of the prison that they can all take, and under attack from zombies, they release a man called Chris from a maximum security cell as he claims he knows the way out. Following a mêlée of attacks, some of the group do manage to escape, and Chris reveals that he is Claire's brother.

Alice manages to get a boat out to Arcadia, but when she boards the ship there's no sign of life. Claire then remembers that when she arrived in Alaska, the convoy she was in was ambushed by Umbrella and placed in mind control devices. She realises that Arcadia is actually a trap by the evil corporation to lure the non-infected to them, so they can perform experiments on them.

Alice finds Wesker on the boat and he reveals that the virus has given him special powers, but that he's struggling to control it. In order to keep control he must eat human DNA, but this scared the Umbrella employees away. He believes that by eating Alice, he can finally gain control of the virus. He attacks her but she survives, forcing him to retreat by plane. He then attempts to detonate a bomb on Arcadia, but Alice planted it on the plane, blowing it up.

The film ends with a figure parachuting from the plane, and it is revealed that Jill Valentine, who went missing in the previous movie, is now also wearing a mind control device.

RESIDENT EVIL: APOCALYPSE (2004)

The second movie in the Resident Evil series picks up where the first film left off. Alice is trapped in Raccoon City, sealed off by the Umbrella Corporation to keep the zombies that have escaped from the Hive and the infected citizens at bay.

Having been experimented on, Alice has superhuman strength as the T-virus has bonded with her. She's not the only one fighting against the zombies. During the evacuation of the city, the virus starts infecting some of the citizens, so Umbrella worker Timothy Cain seals the last exit, and orders the soldiers to fire warning shots at the crowd, forcing them back into the infected city. Umbrella's Special Tactics and Rescue Squad (S.T.A.R.S.) is inside the city, trying to take control, but the growing number of zombies becomes too powerful for them and members of the team start to become infected by the attackers. Alice manages to save a couple of the team, along with a news reporter.

To take control of the worsening situation, Umbrella releases its Nemesis program to kill the remaining S.T.A.R.S. team members and the roaming zombies. When Dr Charles Ashford, an Umbrella scientist and creator of the T-virus, realises that the company is planning to drop a nuclear weapon on the city, he bargains with Alice that he'll save her if she can rescue his daughter. The group manage to get to his daughter, fighting off zombie dogs and children along the way, but the scientist is captured by Major Cain. In order to save Dr Ashford, and in turn herself and the group, Alice is forced by the Major to fight the Nemesis creature. She overpowers it, but before killing it realises that it's Matt from the first film. The pair team up and attack the Umbrella troops, but Matt is killed. The others manage to escape the city by helicopter before the city is nuked.

Alice is recaptured by Umbrella and taken to another research facility where she is kept in a water tank. She manages to fight her way out, and is rescued by the group disguised as employees, who pull up in an SUV with an order to take her into custody. As the group drive away, we see Umbrella scientist Dr Isaacs saying: 'Program Alice activated' and the camera zooms into Alice's eye to show a flashing Umbrella logo.

RESIDENT EVIL: EXTINCTION (2007)

The third in the Resident Evil series is set five years after the dreaded T-virus broke out in Raccoon City. The movie starts with Alice back at the mansion from the first instalment. She manages to make her way past various obstacles and traps, but is eventually killed. When her body is dumped outside in a pit, hundreds of clones form!

The T-virus has now spread around the world. Alice remains a priority for the Umbrella Corporation's head of research Dr Isaacs, and catching her in the wasteland that was once North America is his main focus. However, he's under orders from the new management to use clones of Alice rather than attempt her recapture, even though he thinks her blood will lead to a cure.

Alice isn't the only one roaming the desolate US. When she encounters a convoy of Raccoon City survivors under attack from infected birds, she uses her psionic powers to fill the sky with a raging fire, thereby saving them. Alice is introduced to Claire Redfield, the woman leading the convoy, who tells her of an infection-free area in Alaska, as pointed to in a diary she found. Alice and Carlos, another one of the survivors, convince Claire to lead the convoy to the 'clean' area, so they prepare to go to Las Vegas to stock up on supplies for the journey.

Meanwhile, Isaacs has been working on a solution to control the zombies, but rather than subduing them, he creates a new breed. Using her powers, Alice leads the Umbrella organisation to her whereabouts, and Isaacs is ordered to send the new zombies from his experiments to intercept the convoy. Most of the convoy die in the attack, but Alice manages to overpower Umbrella's attempts to shut her down. After finding the now infected Isaacs, she uses his computer to locate Umbrella's underground facility.

When the convoy arrives at the facility they find the entrance swarming with zombies. Carlos sacrifices himself, driving a truck into the zombies and blowing himself up. This gives the others time to get into a helicopter to escape, with Alice staying behind. She enters the facility, where she discovers that her blood is the cure to the T-virus. Following a battle with the mutated Isaacs, Alice's clone saves her from the laser that kills Isaacs.

The movie closes with a hologram of Alice telling the Umbrella board in Tokyo that she and her hundreds of clones are coming for them!

THE RETURN OF THE LIVING DEAD (1985)

The first in the series of Living Dead movies directed by Dan O'Bannon, *The Return of the Living Dead* stars Clu Gulager as Burt, James Karen as Frank, Don Calfa as Ernie and Thom Mathews as Freddy.

At the start of the movie, Frank, a foreman, is working at the Uneeda Medical Supply warehouse, which is next door to the local cemetery. Frank is trying to impress Freddy, who has just joined his team. He shows him a container containing a mummified corpse from an experiment the US army did in the warehouse, but also manages to release the toxic gas within the container – and the corpse.

The gas gets outside the building and the graves in the cemetery start to open as the corpses come alive as zombies. Frank and Freddy are affected too and start to feel extremely ill. Their friends in the warehouse have to fight the zombies but it looks like an impossible task as the zombies are so strong and so fast. They start to attack people outside the warehouse and some punks have to try to stop them killing everyone.

The movie was based on the novel of the same name by John Russo. John had co-written the script for the 1968 movie *Night of the Living Dead* with George A Romero, who also directed it. They decided to part ways after the movie was released and John was given the rights to any future movie that contained the words

'Living Dead', meaning that George could not make any more of that ilk.

John was extremely excited about *The Return of the Living Dead* being made and Tobe Hooper – best known for directing the Texas Chainsaw Massacre movies and *Salem's Lot* – was hired as director. He ended up pulling out because he was offered the movie *Lifeforce*, so Dan O'Bannon was given the job. Dan had already been hired to work on the script so he knew the movie inside out. He ended up changing the script quite a bit because he wanted to bring his own identity to it. He used dialogue you wouldn't expect and more sex and nudity than appear in the George A Romero movies.

RETURN OF THE LIVING DEAD PART II (1988)

The second movie in Dan O'Bannon's Living Dead series, *Return of the Living Dead Part II*, was directed by Ken Wiederhorn. The family in the movie shares the same surname as Burt in the first movie. Michael Kenworthy plays Jesse Wilson, Marsha Dietlein plays Lucy Wilson, Dana Ashbrook plays Tom Essex and James Karen plays Ed.

The opening scene features soldiers smoking marijuana as they transport large barrels of trioxin. One of the barrels falls off its truck and into the river, but the soldiers are oblivious. The next day three boys find it.

The boys are playing in a cemetery and decide to lock Jesse in one of the mausoleums. The two bullies then decide to open the barrel and the toxic gas is released into the atmosphere. Some grave robbers arrive and when they get to the mausoleum they free Jesse, who runs home. Ed, Brenda and Joey are only interested in stealing anything of value from the graves.

Later that day Jesse heads over to the home of Billy, one of the boys who locked him in the mausoleum. When Jesse get to Billy's house he is told that Billy is really ill. Jesse is briefly allowed in and finds out from Billy that the illness was caused by exposure to the trioxin. Before Jesse leaves, Billy makes him promise that he won't tell anyone that the reason he's ill is because he opened the barrel. On his way home Jesse is attacked by a zombie covered in tar but he manages to get away. He takes a short cut through the cemetery but the dead have started to rise from their graves and a zombie's hand grabs him from a grave when he runs past.

The grave robbers come under attack and try to fight back with a crowbar but end up running for their lives. They bump into Billy's parents and warn them about the zombies. Jesse makes it home but his sister Lucy is angry that he went out and has a go at him. Once he's safe in his bedroom he calls the military using the phone number he saw printed on the barrel they found. He's placed on hold...

Ed, Brenda and Joey need to get out of town so they steal a van belonging to cable technician Tom, who is currently working in Jesse's home. They are so keen to make their escape that they hit a zombie. The zombie falls into a telegraph pole, cutting off Jesse's call to the military. Billy's dad sees what the trio have done and threatens them with a gun, only to be killed by a zombie. His wife sees it happen and tries to run away but her husband reanimates and kills her.

Everywhere Ed, Brenda and Joey look they see zombies, so they rush to Jesse's house to take cover and think of a plan. Jesse tells them his neighbour Dr Mandel might be able to help them escape. They head to his house with Tom and Lucy but are ambushed by zombies and just manage to escape in the doctor's car. The group hit many zombies as they try to escape and one ends up on their roof. He tries to attack them but they cut his hand off with the car's window. The severed hand then tries to attack them but they throw it out of the window.

Joey and Ed have started displaying the symptoms Billy had. They make it to the hospital but it is deserted. Tom, Lucy and Jesse go to get more weapons while Dr Mandel tells Brenda that Ed and Joey are going to die, but she can't accept this and goes to leave with them. They are stopped by three soldiers but Ed attacks one of them and the others drive off quickly. As Ed tucks into the soldier's brains, Brenda and Joey leave. When they get in the car Joey turns into a zombie and attacks Brenda, but she manages to escape. Another zombie goes for her but she rips his jaw off and runs into a nearby church. Joey follows her and confesses that he loves her but he wants to eat her too. Brenda knows she can't get away and succumbs.

Tom, Lucy, Jesse and Dr Mandel come up with a plan to save the town from the zombies. They will use frozen brains from the hospital to get the zombies to follow them to the town's power plant and then drop the brains in water. They will have wired up electricity cables to each puddle so when the zombies touch the brains in the water, they will be electrocuted.

Billy is now a zombie and lets the other zombies into the site before Jesse and the group are ready. Tom and Lucy hide in the truck but Jesse is inside the power plant. Billy tries to kill Jesse but Jesse manages to stop him by stabbing him with a screwdriver. Jesse then triggers the power, electrocuting all the zombies, but Billy returns for round two, with the screwdriver Jesse used to stab him. He pushes Jesse into a control panel but a huge transformer falls through the roof, giving Dr Mandel enough time to get Billy's attention by telling him his fly is open. Jesse and the doctor then push Billy into the transformer, killing him.

DID YOU KNOW?

One of the zombies was dressed up to resemble a zombie in Michael Jackson's music video 'Thriller'. At the end of the movie this character pulls off some Michael Jackson dance moves to add some comedy value.

RETURN OF THE LIVING DEAD 3 (1993)

Return of the Living Dead 3 was written by John Penney and directed by Brian Yuzna, who also directed the zombie movies *Bride of Re-Animator* and *Beyond Re-Animator*. Although this was the third in Dan O'Bannon's Living Dead series, it is very different from the first two, which had slapstick elements. It was the least popular of all the Living Dead movies.

The movie starts with Curt Reynolds (J Trevor Edmond) stealing his dad's security pass for the military base where he works. He doesn't want to but he'll do anything his girlfriend Julie (Melinda Clarke) asks him to. They head there and once inside witness experiments on a corpse.

The military hope that by using the toxic gas trioxin they can create soldiers from dead people. Curt's dad Colonel John Reynolds (Kent McCord), Colonel Peck

(James T Callahan) and Lieutenant Colonel Sinclair (Sarah Douglas) are given the task of training the zombies, but this is proving to be extremely difficult. Sinclair wants to put the zombies into skeletal amour so when they are not needed for military operations they can be controlled, shut down and locked away.

John has a different idea: he wants to use 'paretic infusion' to freeze the zombies' brains. They test this theory by shooting a zombie in the head with a chemical designed to paralyse it, but the chemical wears off too quickly and the zombie attacks the doctor, biting his fingers off then killing him violently. The doctor becomes a zombie and attacks a colleague before he is stopped. The room is sealed and John is told he is being moved off the project and will be transferred to a base in Oklahoma. Sinclair is to take over control of the project.

John returns home to inform his family that they are moving but Curt reacts badly. He is sick of having to move constantly because of his dad's job. He jumps on his motorbike and rides off. Julie tries to touch his crotch as he's driving, which causes him to lose control of the bike. They nearly hit a truck but he manages to swerve. They crash and Julie dies from a broken neck.

Injured and emotional, Curt can't bear to think of his life without Julie. He takes her body to the military base, lets himself in with his father's key card and gives her some trioxin gas to reincarnate her. Julie seems relatively normal at first but then starts to crave human flesh.

A short time later Julie and Curt go to a grocery store but trouble erupts between a gang and the owner. The gang shoot at the owner and he dies. Julie can't help herself and tucks in. She infects one of the gang members and he becomes a zombie too. Curt and Julie are chased through the city and then Julie decides to commit suicide. Before she does, they meet a homeless man called Riverman who hides them in the sewers.

Back at the base, the military have found out about Curt breaking into the site and want to get their hands on Julie so they can experiment on her. She tries to stop herself wanting to eat people by self-harming. The gang catch up with them but she kills many of them and then kills Riverman. The military arrive and take them away.

Curt and Julie think they have been saved, but Sinclair separates them and takes Julie away. Curt manages to free her but the other zombie specimens escape too. Sinclair puts Riverman in lockable skeletal amour but he manages to overpower it and kills her. Her method was no better than John's at controlling the zombies.

Riverman could kill Curt and Julie too but he doesn't, although Curt is bitten by another zombie as they try to get out. Curt and Julie don't want to live as zombies and go to the town's crematorium to die together in the furnace.

RETURN OF THE LIVING DEAD: NECROPOLIS (2005)

Return of the Living Dead: Necropolis was the fourth movie in Dan O'Bannon's Living Dead series. The director was Ellory Elkayem.

The movie begins with a man called Charles Garrison (Peter Coyote) doing a deal with some Russians in a power station. He has been sent to Chernobyl to collect six containers of trioxin 5. During the exchange one of the Russians gets trioxin on his hands and turns into a zombie. He kills his partner but before he gets the chance to kill Charles, Charles blasts him in the head.

Charles is the uncle and guardian of Julian (John Keefe) and Jake Garrison, two boys whose parents died the year before. They are out on their motorbikes when their friend Zeke (Elvin Dandel) is injured. They rush him to hospital but he dies from an allergic reaction to painkillers. His body is taken to Hybra Tech, a place where experiments are carried out on corpses. Julian is determined to get his friend's body out of there.

It turns out that Charles has been experimenting with the trioxin gas and reanimated a rat by accident, which went on to kill two homeless men. He finds Julian, Jake and their friends inside Hybra Tech when they sneak in and he agrees to their requests and takes them to Zeke.

Zeke's corpse is in a room full of zombie clones. Charles reveals that the boys' parents are not actually dead, which is a shock to Julian. In an attempt to deactivate the building's alarm, Julian's friend Katie (Jana Kramer) releases a horde of zombies and Julian goes to find his mum and dad.

Zeke's corpse is bitten by a zombie so he reanimates and tries to eat his friends. Julian finds his parents but they are 'über-soldiers' now, not the people he remembers. Charles releases Julian's parents but they will all have to fight the zombies if they are to get out alive. It looks like Julian will be killed by the zombies but Katie arrives in a truck and the friends climb aboard. Jake saves Becky's life but is killed by a zombified Zeke.

The truck comes under fire from the boys' parents and Zeke but they manage to kill Julian's mum and former friend. Suddenly a SWAT team arrives, annihilating any remaining zombies. Julian's dad appears and shoots Katie in the head but is then killed by a member of the SWAT team.

Charles makes a quick exit with the remaining barrels of trioxin so he can use them in future experiments. The movie finishes with a news reporter revealing that there was a zombie attack at Hybra Tech but the company denies that there was. The reporter is then attacked and killed by a zombie.

RETURN OF THE LIVING DEAD: RAVE TO THE GRAVE (2005)

The fifth and final movie of the Living Dead series was *Return of the Living Dead: Rave to the Grave*, directed by Ellory Elkayem. Aimee-Lynn Chadwick played Becky, Cory Hardrict played Cody, John Keefe played Julian Garrison and Jenny Mollen played Jenny. The movie was filmed in Romania and the Ukraine.

For this movie the characters from the fourth movie reappear. It is a year since the zombie incident at Hybra Tech and the friends are now college freshmen. Fellow students are using a party drug processed from trioxin to get high at a rave, but when they take too much they turn into zombies. The friends see students who have reanimated, but they just think they are in fancy dress for Halloween and carry on enjoying themselves until things turn nasty. The zombies attack and they are in a nightmare situation again. It takes a long time for armed police to arrive, by which time only a few people are left alive.

REVENGE OF THE ZOMBIES/THE CORPSE VANISHED (1943)

Revenge of the Zombies is a classic zombie movie and was released in 1943. It was directed by Steve Sekely and starred John Carradine as Dr Max Heinrich von Altermann, Gale Storm as Jennifer Rand and Robert Lowery as Larry Adams. It was the first ever zombie Nazi movie.

The movie centres around Dr Max Heinrich von Altermann, who is a scientist trying to create zombie fighters for the Nazis. He turns his dead wife into a zombie but she tries to stop him controlling her.

ROMERO, GEORGE A

George Andrew Romero is considered by many to be the 'Godfather of all Zombies' as he virtually created the zombie genre within horror movies. He is an American–Canadian screenwriter and director who was born on 4 February 1940 in New York but became a Canadian citizen in 2009 after living in Toronto for a long time. His father was born on the Caribbean island of Cuba to Spanish parents and his mother's family are Lithuanian and American.

George's passion for horror movies started after he graduated from Carnegie Mellon University in

Pittsburgh. He had started his career filming adverts and short films, but when he filmed a man having his tonsils removed in a scene for the show *Mister Rogers' Neighborhood* he decided that making horror movies would be fun. He set up Image Ten Productions with his friends and he wrote, directed and edited his first full-length horror movie, *Night of the Living Dead*, which was released in 1968.

That was followed by *There's Always Vanilla* in 1971 – the only romantic comedy he has ever done (he considers it one of his worst movies). In 1973 he brought out *The Crazies*, a horror movie exploring what happens when a biological weapon is accidentally released on an American town. The infected people become the 'crazies', start attacking the soldiers and go insane. Many people have wrongly said it is a zombie movie, but the crazies are very much alive.

George's next zombie film was *Dawn of the Dead* in 1978. He then did several more horror movies before *Day of the Dead* was released in 1985. In 1990 George reunited with Dario Argento, with whom he had worked on *Dawn of the Dead*, to do *Two Evil Eyes*, which consisted of two tales based on the writings of Edgar Allan Poe. George and Dario directed one story each. A few months later, in October 1990, a remake of *Night of the Living Dead* was released. It was directed by Tom Savini but George rewrote the screenplay, helped to produce it and hired some of the crew members from his 1968 movie.

The following year George had an uncredited cameo in Jonathan Demme's *Silence of the Lambs*, playing an FBI agent in Memphis, and in 1993 he directed and wrote *The Dark Half* and in 2000 *Bruiser*. In 2004 a remake of *Dawn of the Dead* was made, directed by Zack Snyder. The following year *Land of the Dead* came out, the fourth in the Dead series. George was the director, writer and editor of the movie.

In 2007 George released *Diary of the Dead*, the fifth movie in the Dead series, but it wasn't a straightforward follow-on movie. It was a reboot, 'a rejigging of the myth'. Two years later *Survival of the Dead* was released but fans and critics didn't rate it as highly as the previous movies in the series.

As well as directing movies George has also directed adverts. In 1998 he directed a very successful one for the video game *Resident Evil 2*. In it he had the two main characters, Claire Redfield and Leon S Kennedy, fight zombies at a police station. George was the perfect man for the job because the game's designers had been influenced by his movies when designing how the zombies would look, feel and behave.

DID YOU KNOW?

George's favourite movie of all time is *The Tales of Hoffmann*, a 1951 opera-ballet British movie, directed by Michael Powell and Emeric Pressburger.

George will often have a cameo in his movies. In his zombie movies he has played a Washington reporter in *Night of the Living Dead*, a TV director in *Dawn of the Dead*, a zombie in *Day of the Dead*, a puppeteer in *Land of the Dead* and a police chief in *Diary of the Dead*.

George wrote a script for the first *Resident Evil* movie but it was never used, as the people making the movie decided they preferred a script written by Paul WS Anderson.

George planned to have his own zombie game called *City of the Dead* but it was never finished because the company he was making it with fell into financial difficulties.

One of George's unused zombie movie scripts was used for a graphic novel mini-series called *Toe Tags* (aka *The Death of Death*), which was published by DC Comics in 2004. It is the story of Damien, a zombie who has been given an experimental serum that lets him keep his free will and his memory. On the run with his girlfriend, and pursued by both the living and the undead, he has to reconcile his former life with what he is now.

The six-part serial received mixed reviews, with the reviewer from Comicologist.com writing: 'Toe Tags is worth reading if you're interested in exploring the "Dead" universe further, but as a stand-alone story, it's not all that strong.'

Kaustubh Thirumalai from KvltSite.com wrote: 'I don't know why, but I got a feeling that the whole series was on a steep decline from the first issue onwards, in terms of the plot, inking, dialogue, continuity – everything. The story is somewhat painful to follow even though there are not too many characters involved. Surmising, *Toe Tags: The Death of Death* series was a big disappointment, more so because of the very promising first issue (third one was the worst) and 'cause I usually like Romero's stuff. But the series does have a few redeeming qualities. The ending was quite enjoyable with bouts of good action here and there. Plus, the artwork stands out. Tom Castillo does some good work. His action sequences are rather thrilling. I'd recommend this only if you're a bigger Romero fan than a comic fan.'

S IS FOR...

SEVERED: FOREST OF THE DEAD (2005)

Severed: Forest of the Dead was a Canadian horror movie directed by Carl Bessai. The script was written by Julian Clarke and Travis McDonald.

The movie focuses on a clash between a global logging company and a group of environmental activists. The logging company set out to experiment with a small part of the forest to increase their profits by improving their yield of logs. Their experimental procedure goes severely wrong with both workers and activists turning into zombies.

The first zombie is created when one of the

logging team is touched by weeping tree sap after he cuts down a large tree with his chainsaw. Leading members of the corporation become concerned when their workers don't report back and they send Tyler (Paul Campbell), one of the owner's sons, to find out what is going on. When he arrives he finds the site deserted but then sees the zombies. He runs off to find somewhere safe to hide and joins a small group of survivors. The group consists of foreman Mac (Julian Christopher), a protester called Rita (Sarah Lind) and a deranged biologist called Carter (JR Bourne). Tyler questions the scientist about what has happened.

The zombies in this movie are different from the zombies in other movies and are more sinister in appearance. Their skin is yellow and they have large, protruding veins on their foreheads. The only way the group can survive is by decapitating the zombies.

SHAUN OF THE DEAD (2004)

Co-written by British comedy star Simon Pegg and Edgar Wright (who directed the movie), *Shaun of the Dead* is a modern cult classic zombie movie.

The movie was based on the 'Art' episode of the sitcom *Spaced* (also co-written by Simon, who starred in the series, and directed by Edgar). The episode follows Simon's character who, under the influence of amphetamines and the PlayStation game *Resident Evil 2*, hallucinates that he's in the middle of a zombie invasion. It was this, coupled with their love for the classic Dead trilogy by George A Romero, that inspired them to make the movie.

Shaun of the Dead follows Shaun (Simon Pegg), a salesman who spends every night at his local pub, the Winchester, with his best friend Ed (Nick Frost). With no respect at work and a bad relationship with his stepfather, Shaun's life goes from bad to worse when his girlfriend Liz (Kate Ashfield) ends their relationship after he forgets their anniversary.

Shaun heads off to his local with Ed (another no-hoper) to drown his sorrows. After a heavy night of drinking the pair wake to a surprise the following day. TV reports tell of an outbreak of zombies, some of which appear at the house. The friends decide to arm themselves with the contents of the shed and make their way to the safest place they know – the Winchester. They stop off to collect Shaun's mum Barbara, stepfather Philip, Liz and her flatmates – leaving behind Shaun's flatmate Pete who is now a zombie.

Philip dies of a zombie bite but manages a reconciliation with Shaun. Before they make it to the Winchester, the group are forced to abandon the car. They meet a young actress called Yvonne and some more survivors. To make their way past zombies blocking the path to the pub, they pretend to be zombies themselves. The plan works until Ed and Shaun start to bicker, and the zombies begin to attack. Still, they manage to make it to the safety of the Winchester and take cover.

The zombies return to the pub when Ed gives away their position when he wins on the fruit machine. Slightly redeeming himself, Ed gets the Winchester rifle above the bar working and they manage to keep the zombies at bay. Despite this, Barbara is bitten, and David points the rifle at her. Shaun and Ed protest and Barbara's life is spared, but when she returns as a zombie, Shaun shoots her.

Next to die is Liz's flatmate, who, it has been revealed, loves Liz. He's ripped apart by the zombies when they manage to drag him out of the pub. Another flatmate, Dianne, tries to save him but by unbolting the door lets the zombies in.

Ed makes a Molotov cocktail before being bitten by a zombified Pete. Shaun then uses the explosive mixture to ignite the bar while they manage to escape into the cellar. Now cornered, they contemplate suicide but find a service hatch to escape. Shaun and Liz escape, leaving the mortally wounded Ed behind with the rifle, ready to fend off the zombies. The saga ends when the British army arrives, rescuing Shaun, Liz and Yvonne.

The film ends with a catch-up six months after the incident, when everything is back to normal(ish). The surviving zombies are now being used as cheap labour, with Ed living in the shed of Shaun and Liz's house, playing computer games!

DID YOU KNOW?

Shaun of the Dead has made it into many popular movie lists, including the 'Greatest British Films of All Time' (49th) in *Total Film* (2004), the 'Greatest Comedy Film of All Time' (third) in a Channel 4 poll, and one of the 'Top 25 Horror Movies' in *Time* magazine.

SHOCK WAVES (1977)

Shock Waves is a zombie movie directed by Ken Wiederhorn. Some zombie fans might know it by its alternative titles *Death Corps* or *Almost Human*.

The movie tells the story of what happens when a party yacht runs aground on an island off the coast of Florida. The people on the boat see an old freighter and find an old man (Peter Cushing) who used to be an SS Commander in the Second World War. He is joined by his Nazi zombie stormtroopers who were unstoppable during the war as they could kill anyone or anything with their bare hands. They were never captured and had disappeared until now… and the young partygoers must run for their lives!

The movie has become a cult classic and received favourable reviews. The writer for CinePassion.org said: 'The oceanic opening features iridescent gradations of blue and orange and John Carradine as a link to [Steve] Sekely's *Revenge of the Zombies*. The Final Girl (Brooke Adams) is introduced catatonic in a lifeboat adrift, her flashback reveals a gaggle of cranky tourists hoping for "one hell of a yarn" and getting it in an island off the Florida coast, with colonial arches and WWII holdovers amid the foliage. Nazi ghouls ("neither dead nor alive, but somewhere in between") comprise the Wellsian joke, goggle-wearing Aryan mummies engineered by the SS Dr Moreau (Peter Cushing) feebly lording over the marshlands.

'The tone is nightmarishly tranquil, the action moves surreally from beachfront to swamp to darkened swimming pool, claustrophobia gets to the point where even the toughest castaway would rather face the shuffling death squad than stay inside another pressure-cooker chamber. An ineffably ethereal and erudite frisson-fest, which manages to register Santayana's warning while brushing ever so slightly against *Germany Year Zero* (a phonograph forgotten amid a regime's rubble) and *Through a Glass Darkly* (living corpses emerging from the sea and trudging toward the camera).'

SLITHER (2006)

Written and directed by James Gunn, *Slither* combines zombie horror with science fiction and comedy.

The story starts when a meteorite crashes into a small American town. It brings with it a strange egg, which is found by local businessman Grant (Michael Rooker). What he doesn't know is that it contains an alien parasite. This slug-like creature takes over Grant's body, absorbing his consciousness and memories, and changing him into a blob-like monster with an uncontrollable hunger for meat.

The parasite spreads rapidly around the small town, turning almost all its inhabitants into zombies. All the infected townspeople come under the control of Grant, who acts as the 'hive' mind for the walking dead. But the town's inhabitants are not enough for Grant, who plans to infect the whole world. This leaves the fate of the town and possibly the whole human race on the shoulders of a small group of survivors, including Grant's biology teacher wife Starla (Elizabeth Banks) and the local sheriff Bill (Nathan Fillion).

SURVIVAL OF THE DEAD (2009)

An American–Canadian production, George A Romero's *Survival of the Dead* was the sixth movie in his Dead series. The movie begins with Colonel 'Nicotine' Crockett (Alan van Sprang) surrounded by zombie guardsmen after a mission fails and his men get bitten by zombies and reanimate. As a result he loses his rank of colonel and is demoted to sergeant. Because of this, he gathers some troops and decides to flee. Nicotine, Kenny, Francisco and Tomboy stop a group of students and steal their food supplies and firearms. This scene was shown in the 2007 movie *Diary of the Dead*.

On Plum Island, a small island just off the coast of Delaware, two Irish families who have clashed over the years are debating what they should do with zombies. The Muldoons, headed by Seamus Muldoon, have been keeping their undead loved ones alive. The family believe that they will find a cure and be able to bring them back. The O'Flynns, headed by Patrick (Kenneth Welsh), don't believe there is a cure and feel their safety is being jeopardised.

The O'Flynns gather a group of supporters to kill any zombies on the island. The scene ends with Seamus Muldoon and Patrick's daughter Janet (Kathleen Munroe) banishing Patrick O'Flynn and his supporters from the island.

Three weeks later Nicotine and his group of National

Guardsmen are still fighting the zombies who cross their path and have gained a new member called Boy. Boy tells them of Plum Island after seeing a video posted on the internet by Patrick O'Flynn. The group head to the port and come across the O'Flynn clan. The two groups exchange fire while being attacked by zombies at the same time.

While all the action is happening, Francisco manages to find a ferry for the group to travel on and they set off, leaving the O'Flynn clan – minus Patrick – to be killed by the zombies. Patrick calls a truce with Nicotine's group and boards the ferry with them to Plum Island. He explains on the way that he has been encouraging others to go over to the island to annoy Seamus Muldoon. On their journey Francisco, who had an earlier encounter with a zombie and swallowed some of its blood, starts to feel ill.

When the group arrive on the island they get a nasty surprise as all the humans sent over by Patrick have been killed and his daughter Janet has turned into a zombie. The Muldoon clan have kept alive all the remaining zombies and have tied them up in chains. They are put in scenes mimicking what they did when they were alive. Patrick's daughter Janet is riding around on her horse, the mailman is putting mail in the mailbox, and another zombie is chopping wood with an axe.

Patrick heads towards the town in anger; he wants to round up some of his remaining friends and family to help him. In the meantime two of the Muldoon clan attack Nicotine's group, killing Kenny. Patrick walks over and shoots him in the head so he cannot reincarnate as a zombie.

Francisco's sickness gets worse. Fearing he will die and come back as a zombie, he asks Tomboy to shoot him so he can't. Reluctant Tomboy does as she is asked, but is then captured by the Muldoon clan. Boy is helping Nicotine, stitching up his wounds from the earlier attack. Then Patrick's daughter Janet appears and reveals that the zombie they saw on the horse is actually her twin sister Jane. She tells how Jane is the favourite of the two, then helps Boy tend to Nicotine's wounds. Once Nicotine is ready, he agrees to join forces to avenge Kenny's death. The trio find the rest of the O'Flynn clan and plot their attack on the Muldoons.

The bridge across the island's river is the boundary between the clans' lands. A stand-off occurs between the two sides but the O'Flynns and Nicotine are captured by the Muldoons. Boy and Janet manage to escape into the forest. Later the Muldoons decide to release Tomboy and she leaves with the knowledge that Seamus Muldoon's wife has turned into a zombie and is now chained up in their kitchen at home.

The argument between the two clans continues, but

now Seamus wants to prove to Patrick that he is right and that zombies will eat things other than human flesh. He brings out Patrick's daughter Jane to demonstrate his theory by getting her to eat her horse. Seamus's helper Chuck escorts a mass of zombies to the scene so they witness Jane eating the horse, in the hope they will copy her. However, Jane does not eat the horse.

Janet then appears accompanied by Boy and proceeds to give her father, Nicotine and the rest of their group weapons so they can fight back. Jane reaches out for Janet and then bites her. The two families start firing at each other again. Chuck decides to join the O'Flynns but is later killed by Seamus for his betrayal. When he dies the group of zombies break free and eat his body. The fight then takes a turn for the worse as the zombies attack both families, leaving few survivors.

When they each have one bullet left in their guns, Patrick and Seamus decide to call a truce. However, as soon as Patrick turns, Seamus shoots him in the back. As Patrick starts to die he pulls out a hidden gun from his sleeve and kills Seamus. Nicotine and his men have had enough and head back to the ferry to leave the bloodbath island. After they go, Janet sees her twin sister take a bite out of her horse and realises there might be hope for the zombies yet. She runs to the ferry to tell the group but is shot by her father Patrick because he saw that she'd been bitten by her sister.

As the film comes to an end, Nicotine, Boy and Tomboy head back to the mainland on the ferry, swearing they will never turn out like the O'Flynn and Muldoon clans. They go back to their truck, which contains $1 million they seem to have acquired, and head off to start their future as survivors. Back on Plum Island there is a zombie stand-off between Patrick and Seamus, who point their empty guns at each other.

The movie received mainly negative reviews from critics and only managed a score of 29 out of 100 on Rotten Tomatoes (based on 82 reviews). 'Steeped in fan-pleasing gore but woefully thin on ideas, originality (beyond new zombie-offing methods) or directorial flair,' wrote Leslie Felperin from *Variety*. Elias Savada, who reviewed the movie for the webzine *Film Threat*, said: '"A man dies, he gets stupid," someone observes in the film. Maybe if a man makes too many films about the dead, the same fate awaits him. Mr Romero, you are on notice.'

DID YOU KNOW?

The movie was shot in Port Dover and Toronto in Ontario and the cast and crew were almost all Canadian.

The film took its inspiration from the 1958 Western *The Big Country*.

T IS FOR...

THRILLER (1983)

Mention zombies to most people and the first thing that pops into their heads will be Michael Jackson's 'Thriller' video. The video was released on 2 December 1983 and fans around the world were instantly in awe of it.

The storyline starts in a wooded area, with a 1950s Michael and his girl (Ola Ray, a *Playboy* model and actress) returning from a date. In true horror movie style, the car they are travelling in runs out of petrol. At first the girl doesn't believe Michael's story but once they start walking she apologises. He tells her that he hopes she likes him as much as he likes her and after she says she does he asks her to be his girl and presents her with a ring.

He tries to explain that he is different from other guys but as he's speaking the full moon appears and he starts to change. He quickly tells her to get away but she just stands there. He starts convulsing and his body changes to that of a werecat. His girlfriend screams and runs as fast as she can through the woods but he catches up with her. She falls down and just as it looks like he's going to attack her, the camera switches to Michael and his girlfriend watching the story as a movie in a cinema. Michael is clearly enjoying it, but his girlfriend is scared and insists on leaving. Michael reluctantly follows her out.

Once outside, Michael tells her that *Thriller* is only a movie and he knows she's scared. His girlfriend tries to deny it but as they walk home Michael starts to tease her by singing 'Thriller'. It's foggy and as they pass a cemetery the dead start to rise from their graves. Soon the zombies surround Michael and his girlfriend. As they get closer and closer the couple look more and more scared, but when the girl looks at Michael she sees that he's changed into a zombie too. Michael and the zombies do the iconic 'Thriller' dance as Michael sings the chorus.

His girlfriend runs for her life and makes it to a deserted house. She lets herself inside, barricading herself in, but she can't stop them. The zombies smash through the windows and floor as she cowers on a couch. She screams as zombie Michael smashes his way through the door, surrounded by his zombie friends. He reaches out to touch her and she screams, but again the setting changes. Michael is back to normal and the deserted house is now a comfortable home. She was asleep all along.

Michael asks her what the problem is and then says he'll take her home. She smiles as he wraps his arms around her but Michael looks directly at the camera and it is clear that he still has his yellow werecat eyes. An evil laugh hints that things aren't going to end the way Michael's girlfriend wants them to.

As the credits roll the zombies are shown dancing and going back to their graves while a disclaimer appears stating: 'Any similarity to actual events or characters living, dead (or undead) is purely coincidental.'

Strange as it may seem, Michael only made the video because sales of his album were lower than expected. It was his manager Frank DiLeo who came up with the idea of doing a video for the next single 'Thriller' because it would boost sales if fans liked it. The video was directed by John Landis, who also wrote and directed *An American Werewolf in London*, *Twilight Zone: The Movie* and *The Blues Brothers*. John and Michael worked together to come up with the screenplay for 'Thriller' and spent a huge amount of money – $800,000 – on making it.

They filmed the video in Los Angeles at the Palace Theater, and the street scenes were shot at the junction of South Calzona Street and Union Pacific Avenue. The deserted house was a real house in the Angelino Heights area, the second oldest area in the whole of Los Angeles.

Michael told MTV how he and John developed the zombies and came up with their dance. He said: 'My idea was to make this short film with conversation… in the beginning – I like having a beginning and a middle and an ending, which would follow a story. I'm very much involved in the complete making and creating of the piece. It has to be, you know, my soul. Usually, you know, it's an interpretation of the music.

'It was a delicate thing to work on because I remember my original approach was: "How do you make zombies and monsters dance without it being comical?" So I said: "We have to do just the right kind of movement so it doesn't become something that you laugh at." But it just has to take it to another level.

'So I got in a room with [choreographer] Michael Peters, and he and I together kind of imagined how these zombies move by making faces in the mirror. I used to come to rehearsal sometimes with monster make-up on, and I loved doing that. So he and I collaborated and we both choreographed the piece and I thought it should start like that kind of thing and go into this jazzy kind of step, you know. Kind of gruesome things like that, not too much ballet or whatever.'

Thanks in no small part to the much talked-about 14-minute video (epic in scale compared with most pop clips), 'Thriller' went on to become one of the most popular Michael Jackson songs, even though it only managed to achieve number four in the US charts. *Thriller* was also the name of Michael's sixth album, released on 30 November 1982. *Rolling Stone* wrote of it at the time: 'Rather than reheating *Off the Wall*'s agreeably mindless funk, Jackson has cooked up a zesty LP whose up-tempo workouts don't obscure its harrowing, dark messages. Jackson's new attitude gives *Thriller* a deeper, if less visceral, emotional urgency than any of his previous work, and marks another watershed in the creative development of this prodigiously talented performer.'

In 2007, Mike Joseph wrote on PopMatters.com: 'Twenty-five years after *Thriller*'s original release, amidst everything that's gone on in Michael Jackson's crazy, insane, screwed-up life, this album still makes people smile, the grooves still make people dance, and the videos still make people stop and stare in awe. This, folks, is where the mere pop stars get separated from the legends. Times may change, music may change, but *Thriller* is one of those few iconic records whose influence seems to be prevalent no matter the climate.'

The 'Thriller' video went on to win two Grammys and four MTV Music Awards. More than a million people bought a copy, making it the most successful music video ever, according to *Guinness World Records*. Michael also released a special documentary that went behind the scenes of the video. It was shown on MTV and an incredible 9 million copies were sold.

Ever since the video was released, the zombies' dance has been copied in various TV shows and movies, from the zombie comedy horror movie *Return of the Living Dead Part II* to the romantic comedy *30 Going on 13*. A 2007 video clip of 1,500 Filipino prisoners performing the routine in their exercise yard became a viral hit on the internet, getting more than 48 million hits. Even the cast of *Glee* have done their own version, which has been viewed more than 87 million times on YouTube.

DID YOU KNOW?

The red jacket worn by Michael in the video was designed by director John Landis's wife.

The man in charge of making the zombies look as realistic as possible was prosthetics and make-up expert Rick Baker. Rick had won an Oscar for Best Make-up for his work on *An American Werewolf in London* and has picked up the same Oscar six more times since then.

Before the video plays, Michael had a disclaimer appear so that fans wouldn't get the wrong idea. It said: 'Due to my strong personal convictions, I wish to stress that this film in no way endorses a belief in the occult.' He was a Jehovah's Witness at the time.

Michael broke several Guinness world records during his career. One of them was 'Most weeks at the top of the US album charts' (*Thriller* was number one for 37 weeks).

One of the zombies was played by veteran horror actor Vincent Price, who also provided the evil laugh and the voice-over in the song.

Vincent told Johnny Carson's *Tonight Show* that Michael had been a big fan of his and had asked him to take part in the video. He had been given two options – a $20,000 payment or a cut of the

Thriller album sales. He went for the money up front, which was a big mistake – he would have earned millions from the royalties!

28 DAYS LATER (2002)

28 Days Later is a British film directed by Danny Boyle. The screenplay was written by Alex Garland, a critically acclaimed novelist whose previous works include the cult classic *The Beach*. Danny also directed the movie adaptation of that novel in 2000, which starred Leonardo DiCaprio and Robert Carlyle.

At the start of *28 Days Later* animal activists break into a laboratory with the aim of releasing chimpanzees. They have no idea what lies in store for them. Seemingly unaware of the reason why the chimps are in the lab, the angry protesters ignore the desperate pleas of the scientist and begin to free the animals. They become infected with a highly contagious virus that exists in the blood and saliva of the chimps, causing extreme anger and murderous rage.

Fast-forward 28 days and the movie's main character Jim (Cillian Murphy) wakes up from a coma after an accident. He is in an empty hospital and attached to a plethora of monitoring equipment. Unaware of

DAN OLIVER

happenings in the recent past, he scours the hospital but there is no one around, and he begins to wonder if he is the last person on Earth. Jim leaves the empty hospital and makes his way into London. As he walks he looks out for signs of life but there are none. It appears that the rage epidemic has evolved from the chimps and has broken out onto the streets and taken the lives of many millions of citizens.

When Jim reaches a church he finds out exactly why the streets are so empty when he is confronted by a group of zombie-like humans who have been infected by the rage virus. While running for his life, he is saved by Selena and Mark, who have managed to survive the outbreak uninfected. They quickly explain what has happened and Jim realises the nightmare situation he is in.

Shortly afterwards, Mark becomes infected, so Selena and Jim must continue their journey alone. After meeting a father and daughter duo, Frank and Hannah, they embark on a journey in Frank's London cab to a safe house with soldiers and a potential antidote to the infection. They find a country manor house outside Manchester patrolled by the British army soldiers, one of whom is Major Henry West (Christopher Eccleston).

However, the promise of salvation is short-lived. Frank gets killed after becoming infected and when the Major tells Jim about his plans for repopulation, things

take a turn for the worse. Jim attempts to get Selena and Hannah out of the manor house but he is confronted by the Major, who shoots Jim in the stomach.

The final scenes show Jim asleep with a bandage around his stomach in a secluded house in a Highland location. With Selena and Hannah downstairs, Jim awakens to the sound of what appears to be a fighter jet outside. As they rush outside, the overhead shot reveals a message of 'hello' to the oncoming plane.

Screenplay writer Alex Garland took a huge amount of inspiration for the film, most notably from George A Romero's three cult classics, *Night of the Living Dead*, *Dawn of the Dead* and *Day of the Dead*. The scenes that Alex particularly acknowledges include the one in the grocery store and the run-in with infected children. Other inspirational movies he recalls are the film of John Wyndham's *The Day of the Triffids* (1962) and *The Omega Man* (1971), which starred Charlton Heston.

Although they took inspiration from classic zombie movies, Alex and director Danny Boyle also felt that the traditional idea of zombies was outdated. They felt that the fears people had back in the 1960s and 1970s came from different things than they do today – for example, zombies being spawned from nuclear power and then moving at a slow pace with their arms facing forward.

The idea of rage that Alex and Danny created is a more realistic view of the fears people have today. The idea of a virus taking over people's brains was born out of modern mini-epidemics around at the time, such as the anthrax virus, mad cow disease and foot-and-mouth disease. As such, the rage virus doesn't just affect its victims' physical appearance but also alters them psychologically, causing uncontrollable rage. Unlike traditional zombie movies, *28 Days Later* uses the rage virus as a metaphor for modern-day angers, such as road rage, work rage or air rage. The movie simply exaggerates an emotion that every person has inside them.

Rotten Tomatoes gave the movie a score of 88 out of 100. AO Scott from the *New York Times* wrote: 'Mr Boyle, whose other films include *Shallow Grave* and *Trainspotting*, has never been accused of lacking narrative flair or visual style. Rather, he has sometimes been suspected of having too much of both, and of lacking gravity or soul. Those movies, though exciting, could leave a sour aftertaste of cynicism in your mouth. The content of this one is far more extreme; you can almost smell the rotting flesh. But what lingers is a curious sweetness. Mr Boyle has hardly lost his sly, provocative perversity or his ear for the rhythms of unchecked violence, but he does seem to be maturing. It's as if, in contemplating the annihilation of the human race, he has discovered his inner humanist.'

DID YOU KNOW?

An unused alternative ending had only Selena and Hannah in the isolated Highland house. We can assume from this that, in this ending, Jim must have died after being shot by the Major.

The hospital used at the start of the film is a real day hospital, but it isn't open at weekends. This gave the crew the ideal opportunity to shoot in what seemed like a deserted building.

The block of flats where Frank and his daughter Hannah lived was an old derelict building, which has now been demolished.

In order to film the deserted streets of London, the crew requested that the police shut down certain areas of central London at 4am for an hour. During this time, cars and taxis were asked to take an alternative route by some very attractive young girls (one of whom was director Danny Boyle's daughter) to stop drivers getting too annoyed. As predicted, this tactic worked a treat as drivers responded amicably to the requests!

MOVIE MISTAKES

In the scene where Frank gets killed, you can see a soldier standing over his body. If you look to the right when the camera moves away you can see a cameraman and camera.

After Mark kills Mr Bridges, his watch has no blood on it and he doesn't have any bite marks. A few seconds later he has lots of blood and a huge bite on his arm.

In the church scene the zombies have nothing on their heads, but when they are set alight you can see their fireproof hoods as they run after Jim.

28 WEEKS LATER (2007)

The sequel to *28 Days Late, 28 Weeks Later* was written and directed by the Spanish filmmaker Juan Carlos Fresnadillo.

In this movie, Don (Robert Carlyle) and his wife Alice are taking refuge in a cottage outside London while the capital is taken over by the virus. Their son Andy and daughter Tammy are safely away from the carnage as they are on a school trip in Spain. When Don and Alice take in a young boy looking for help, it brings unwanted attention from infected humans in the area. As the couple look to flee the cottage, Alice decides she can't leave the terrified boy on his own, which leaves Don with no option but to run for his life.

Twenty-eight weeks later and US forces have managed to create a safe zone known as District One, a heavily guarded area near London that remains uninfected and under 24-hour surveillance. When Tammy and Andy are admitted to the safe zone, they are reunited with their father who has now become a senior member of District One. After mourning the loss of their mother, the children decide to slip away from the safe zone to try to find something to remember her by. Big mistake!

When they arrive at their house in an abandoned part of London, they find their mother in a weak and dishevelled state, but alive. The American soldiers find Tammy, Andy and Alice and take them back to the safe zone. Upon examining Alice, a US army doctor, Scarlet (Rose Byrne), discovers bite wounds on her body. However, she has not been affected by the virus and seems to have a level of immunity. The medical officer warns that she still has the virus and could pass it to others through her blood or saliva.

When Don finds out that Alice is being kept under surveillance, he finds her to explain his reason for leaving her at the cottage. She tells Don that she loves him and they kiss. The passing of saliva means Alice passes the infection to Don and he becomes filled with rage, savagely killing Alice and several soldiers in the safe zone. The rage virus rears its ugly head as Don begins to infect others and the threat of a mass pandemic is at large once again. The safe zone is put on a code red lockdown.

When Scarlet realises that Andy shares a genetic trait with his mother, she believes that he too may be immune to the virus and therefore a key to future cures. Because of this Scarlet decides to lead both Tammy and Andy away to safety. By this point Don has infected a large number of residents across the safe zone, and has set the whole area into a state of panic. The residents take to the streets of the safe zone and army snipers are ordered to wipe out the whole population on sight.

One of those snipers, Doyle (Jeremy Renner), can't bring himself to kill the uninfected people, and tells Scarlet, Tammy and Andy to flee the safe zone and make their way into London before the area is firebombed. Doyle leads Scarlet, Tammy, Andy and other survivors out of the complex and onto the streets, but little do they know that Don is following them. Doyle makes contact with another soldier named Flynn, a helicopter pilot, who tells Doyle to make their way to Wembley Stadium, where they will be flown to safety across the Channel.

After narrowly avoiding the firebomb in the safe zone, Scarlet, Andy and Tammy manage to start a car and make their way underground in the London tube system in order to get to the stadium. However, Don isn't far behind and ambushes them. He viciously beats

Scarlet to death and bites Andy. Before Don has the chance to kill him, Tammy courageously shoots her father with Doyle's gun.

Like his mother, Andy has been infected by the virus but remains immune to its effects. Both children make their way across London to Wembley Stadium to meet Flynn, the helicopter pilot. He agrees to fly them across the Channel to safety.

The final scene of the film leaves the viewer guessing about the ending and another possible sequel. In the scene we see a crashed helicopter with the radio transmitting the voice of a distressed man with a French accent. Then a group of infected victims flood through a dark tunnel, and when they emerge they run towards the Eiffel Tower. It appears the virus, which had been contained for 28 weeks, has now made its way into France and mainland Europe.

We can presume from the final scene that the children made their way safely across to France, but as Andy was bitten by his father, he could have inadvertently caused an outbreak in mainland Europe. Either that or the infected have somehow managed to find a way from England to France.

Rotten Tomatoes gave the movie a lower score than its predecessor but it still did well, scoring 70 out of 100. Peter Travers from *Rolling Stone* wrote in his review: 'Thematic resonance makes *28 Weeks Later* stick to your nightmares. Hold on for a hell of a ride,' while

Claudia Puig wrote in her review for *USA Today*: 'Relentlessly grim and grisly, *28 Weeks Later* is not for the faint of heart. But its provocative post–apocalyptic theme makes for a smart and deeply unsettling film.'

DID YOU KNOW?

The Millennium Stadium in Cardiff had to be used as a double for Wembley Stadium in London. At the time of filming, Wembley was still undergoing reconstruction. When filming the interior scenes, visual effects were used to change the seats in the stadium to the relevant colours.

Director Danny Boyle has hinted at the possibility of a third movie, possibly named *28 Months Later*, which would move the story on further.

MOVIE MISTAKES

When the snipers are told 'all targets are free' you can see the actors they shoot are wearing padding under their clothes to protect them from injury when they fall down.

Ten minutes and 24 seconds into the movie, when Don jumps into the boat, you can see a cameraman sitting in the boat with him.

When Doyle's hands are on fire, you can see that he is wearing fireproof gloves.

TWO EVIL EYES (1990)

In 1990 George A Romero reunited with Dario Argento, with whom he had worked on *Dawn of the Dead*, to do this movie, which is made up of two short stories by the horror writer Edgar Allan Poe.

The first tale was 'The Facts in the Case of M. Valdemar', which tells the story of a man who has a terminal illness and his devious wife Jessica who has a doctor hypnotise him so they can get their hands on his money. The lawyer of the dying man is suspicious when he gets a phone call from Mr Valdemar saying that he wants his wife to have his assets, and so the lawyer tells Jessica that Mr Valdemar must be alive for three more weeks or he will alert the authorities. The next day Mr Valdemar goes into cardiac arrest while under hypnosis, and because his wife and the doctor can't afford to have people finding out he has died, they put his body in the freezer in the basement.

That night Jessica hears noises coming from the basement but she can't wake up the doctor because he has hypnotised himself so he can get a good night's sleep. The next morning they both hear the moaning and when they open the freezer they hear Mr Valdemar speaking from his corpse. He says that his soul is trapped between the living and the dead because he was under hypnosis when he died. He's in a kind of void and there are evil spirits who want to use him so they can be in the living world.

Mr Valdemar orders the doctor to wake him from his hypnosis but Jessica is freaked out and shoots the corpse. She thinks they should bury him quickly and get as far away as possible. The doctor goes outside to dig a grave but Mr Valdemar rises from the freezer and tells Jessica that the evil spirits are using him. She shoots at him again but he grabs her and shoots her in the head.

The doctor decides to free him from the hypnosis but Mr Valdemar warns him it is too late and his body is under the control of the spirits. The doctor does it anyway and Mr Valdemar finally dies properly. The doctor takes what money he can from the house and goes to his own apartment. He uses hypnotism to put himself in a deep sleep but the evil spirits have followed him and kill him. They will use his body as their new vessel.

A few days later policemen arrive at the apartment to investigate some noises that the doctor's neighbours have been hearing and a strange smell. The doctor's rotting corpse attacks one of the policemen, telling him there is no one to wake him up.

The second tale was called 'The Black Cat' and was

directed by Dario Argento. The story is about Rod, a professional crime-scene photographer whose sensitive girlfriend Annabel likes to talk about superstition and witches. When she brings home a stray black cat, Rod takes against it. The growing dislike is mutual. Rod kills the cat and photographs it for his book of horror pictures, but after an argument with Annabel over its disappearance, he has a nightmare about being executed for the murder of a cat in a medieval pagan gathering.

When a barmaid gives Rod a replacement cat, it is identical to the one he killed, even down to the white patch which seems to resemble the shape of a gallows. Rod is determined to do away with the cat for good; when Annabel tries to protect it, he kills her, inventing elaborate lies to explain her disappearance. As suspicions mount, the police visit the flat. At first they find nothing, but, after the cat's kittens give the game away, they discover Annabel's body in a false wall. Rod kills the policemen and tries to escape through a window but accidentally strangles himself with his getaway rope – the nightmare he had was a premonition. The movie closes with the black cat showing up to stare at the sight.

U IS FOR...

UNDEAD (2003)

Written and directed by brothers Michael and Peter Spierig, *Undead* is a combination of comedy and horror. The film tells the story of the serene Australian fishing village of Berkeley, which experiences a bombardment of meteorites, turning the life of its inhabitants upside down.

The movie begins with local beauty queen Rene (Felicity Mason) and her attempt to leave her hometown after losing the family farm to the bank. Rene's plans are halted when the town is suddenly hit by a torrent of strange meteors. But it's not the light display that disrupts the quaint place – the meteor shower results in the inhabitants turning into zombies.

Rene is lucky and escapes turning into one of the living dead. Along with four other survivors, she takes shelter in the home of Marion (Mungo McKay). Marion has had a troubled past, believing that he had been abducted by aliens. Luckily for the survivors, he took self-protection seriously and is the owner of a large collection of guns and a fallout shelter in his basement. Unfortunately for the group, his shelter doesn't have any provisions, so they're forced to venture outside to gather food.

The only option the small group have is to try to flee the hellish town and its population of flesh-hungry zombies. But when they try to escape they're stopped by a huge barrier surrounding the town. The apparently unhinged Marion blames the barrier on the same aliens that abducted him previously.

The group later find out that Marion's suspicions of alien involvement are true! In fact the aliens are trying to stop the zombie infestation, spraying a chemical on the town that was first thought to be acid rain, and then lifting survivors into suspended animation above the cloud top. The alien intervention looks to have worked, and the survivors leave, unaware that one infected resident managed to escape and on his return starts the zombie outbreak again, with Marion as his first victim.

The movie ends back at Rene's repossessed farm,

where she and the survivors have managed to round up and fence in the zombies, under armed guard, waiting for the aliens to return once again with their cure.

DID YOU KNOW?

Most of the special effects were created by the directors on their home computers.

V IS FOR...

VERSUS (2000)

Co-written (with Yûdai Yamaguchi) and directed by Ryûhei Kitamura on a low budget, *Versus* combines mobster violence, vengeful zombies and past lives, all set in the present day. It stars Tak Sakaguchi as KSC2-303.

When high-security prisoner KSC2-303 and his cellmate manage to escape, they arrange to meet up with a group of Yakuza gangsters in the ominous-sounding Forest of Resurrection, to be taken to safety. What the prisoners don't realise is that the forest is the location of one of the world's 666 portals to the other side.

A stand-off ensues between the prisoners and the mobsters over a girl they've brought to the forest as a hostage. Bullets fly and KSC2-303's cellmate and one of the Yakuza are killed — but not for long! The dead Yakuza man immediately returns from death and starts trying to kill his mob friends. They manage to survive his attack, knocking him to the ground in a shower of bullets, but the mysterious battle has just begun.

The forest has been a dumping ground for bodies of victims of the mob for years, but suddenly their victims start to rise from the dead and attack them. Amid all the action, KSC2-303 and the hostage escape into the forest. The head of the Yakuza starts speaking in a strange way about the power within the Forest of Resurrection and, when he catches up with the runaways, KSC2-303 starts remembering his past life and a past conflict with this man.

The prisoner realises that he's involved in much more than a battle with the mob, and it is his destiny to protect the girl from evil. He is actually involved in an age-old conflict recurring through their reincarnations.

The movie ends without a conclusion. The story has it that its makers were hoping to engineer a sequel. Some extra footage was shot and appears on a special edition DVD of *Versus*, but as yet there's no sign of the hoped-for sequel.

DID YOU KNOW?

Hideo Kojima, producer and director of the famous *Metal Gear Solid* video games, was an extra in *Versus*.

THE VIDEO DEAD (1987)

Written, directed and produced by Robert Scott, *The Video Dead* is a horror movie. Robert is most famous for his work as the assistant director on the successful TV series *House* and *Heroes*.

At the start of the movie a writer gains a TV set after one is delivered to his house. The writer didn't order it but is happy to accept the free gift. It doesn't work properly, though, and the only thing it plays is a movie called *Zombie Blood Nightmare*. Then zombies step out of the set into the writer's house. They murder the writer and go to explore the rest of the house.

After the writer's funeral, the house is sold to an unsuspecting family. The mother and father have been living abroad for many years so they don't know the history of the house. They send their teenage children Jeff and Zoe ahead of them to start unpacking while they settle a few matters in Saudi Arabia. Jeff and Zoe explore the house and find the TV in the attic. Jeff turns it on when he's stoned and a woman steps out of the TV and seduces him. She is extremely good-looking but Jeff doesn't believe she is real – he just thinks it's the drugs.

He thinks the weed he has is dodgy so he chucks it down the toilet and puts the TV in the basement. The zombies start exploring the neighbourhood and start killing the neighbours. They kidnap April, the girl who lives next door, and it is down to Jeff and Zoe to save her. They join forces with a man who knows how to fight the zombies but it's not going to be easy.

CraveOnline.com wrote in their review of the movie: 'Yes, *The Video Dead* is the kind of horror comedy that actually makes with the horror, and although the Casio-laden soundtrack does the terror no favours, the script by director Robert Scott is clever and occasionally genuinely affecting: characters you like will die, there's a surprisingly heart-breaking bit where April is so distraught by the memories of her dead loved ones that she brushes her teeth until they bleed, and Roxanna Augesen's performance in the climax is impressive, comprehending as she does the nightmarish quality of her situation while simultaneously rising to meet the challenge. It's a tricky balance, and although her smile is wide enough to make *London After Midnight* comparisons, it's a shame we never saw more of her. Like her co-star Rocky Duvall, she never made another film.

'*The Video Dead* is the kind of clever horror novelty that really should have developed a cult following by now. Not quite as good as *Night of the Creeps* but worthy of being mentioned within the same sentence, *The Video Dead* is full of knowing novelties, like when Jeff gets so excited at the prospect of dismembering zombies that he actually campaigns for the job. Actually, even the zombie dismembering is remarkable: early in the film one of the living dead gets its head caved in with a household iron and thinks nothing of it. Destroying the brain doesn't work, chopping up the body doesn't work, nothing works because this is that rare zombie movie that owes little-to-nothing to the works of George Romero. These suckers are dead, damn it. "Killing" them won't help matters.'

W IS FOR...

THE WALKING DEAD (2010)

The Walking Dead is an American TV series that premiered on Halloween 2010. It became a record-breaker straight away, with 5.3 million people tuning in to see the first episode. It went on to break viewing records in more than 100 countries. There were only six episodes but in November 2010 the AMC network commissioned a second series with 13 episodes. Usually this would have been very risky because only a couple of episodes had aired, but the network was impressed with the way audiences had responded to it and wanted a second series as soon as possible.

Charlie Collier, the President of AMC, told the press: 'The *Dead* has spread! No other cable series has ever attracted as many adults 18–49 as *The Walking Dead*. This reaffirms viewers' hunger for premium television on basic cable. We are so proud to be bringing back the *Dead* again, across the globe.' Sharon Tal Yguado, SVP Scripted Programming, added: 'I wish all programming decisions were no-brainers like this one. *The Walking Dead* is a TV masterpiece on so many levels. We want at least 10 seasons, if not more. Kudos to AMC!'

The Walking Dead is based on *The Walking Dead* comic books, which were developed by Robert Kirkman, Charlie Adlard and Tony Moore. The series centres on a man called Rick Grimes, who wakes up after a zombie apocalypse has taken place. He leads a group of survivors who try to escape the zombies by travelling across the USA to safety. They call the zombies 'walkers'.

In the first episode Rick Grimes (Andrew Lincoln) is trying to find some petrol. He is a sheriff's deputy and as he searches he comes across a young girl. He has no option but to shoot her in the head as she is a walker and will kill him otherwise. After waking from a coma, he is trying to survive in a world filled with walkers.

A flashback shows what happened to him: he was shot in the line of duty and nearly lost his life. He woke up in a deserted hospital with no idea about what was going on. He goes home but finds his house empty; there's no sign of his wife or his son. He thinks they must still be alive because the photo albums are missing from the house. He doesn't know what to do and starts hallucinating. He finds a man called Morgan and his son Duane who are hiding from the walkers in their home. He also learns that the CDC (the Centre for Disease Control) has set up a quarantine zone in Atlanta.

Rick doesn't want to stay put, so after giving Morgan and Duane some guns and a walkie-talkie, he leaves. He thinks his wife Lori (Sarah Wayne Callies) and son Carl (Chandler Riggs) will be in Atlanta so he wants to head there. In fact Lori, Carl and Rick's old partner and best friend Shane (Jon Bernthal) are with a group of survivors not far from the quarantine zone. They have no idea that Rick has woken from his coma and Lori has started a relationship with Shane.

Rick manages to make it to Atlanta on horseback. The city seems empty at first but turns out to be infested with walkers. When he comes under attack he is forced to lock himself in a nearby army tank. He has no way of escaping but then he hears a voice on the radio saying: 'Hey you, dumbass! Yeah, you in the tank. Cozy in there?'

In the second episode Rick is able to escape the walkers with the help of the man who spoke to him on the radio. Glenn is one of a group of survivors and takes

Rick back to meet them. They are hiding out in a department store and are less than pleased when they see that Glenn has brought someone with him, because the walkers will have heard his gunshots. The group are already struggling to deal with conflict between a racist called Merle and a black man called T–Dog. They need to join together if they are to survive, and to settle things down they decide to handcuff Merle to a pipe on the building's roof.

The walkers are soon trying to get to them, so they radio for help. They were sent as a scavenger team from the group that Lori, Carl and Shane belong to, but the main group decide that they can't help them. It looks like they will all be wiped out until Rick and Glenn come up with a plan. They realise that they might be able to trick the walkers into thinking they are walkers too by smothering themselves in a walker's blood and guts. They manage to make it to a van and Glenn creates a diversion. He jumps into a car and sets off the alarm so the walkers will follow him. The rest of the group manage to escape but they leave Merle behind. T–Dog accidentally drops the key to the handcuffs down the drain and thinks he has sealed Merle's fate.

In the third episode, the scavenger team reunite with the main group of survivors and Rick finally sees his wife and son again. However, he decides he must go back to rescue Merle and take back his walkie-talkie and guns that he left behind. He doesn't want Morgan and Duane to make the mistake of going to Atlanta because they will be killed. Shane doesn't think he should go but Rick goes anyway.

Glenn, T-Dog and Daryl (Merle's younger brother) join Rick and together they head for the department store. Back at the camp, Lori breaks things off with Shane; he had lied to her and told her that Rick had died. She would never have started a relationship with him otherwise. Shane really loves her and is devastated when she warns him to stay away from her family. He takes out his frustrations on Ed, a wife-beater who is part of the group with his wife Carol, and nearly kills him.

When the rescue party get to the roof of the department store, Rick is shocked to find that Merle is nowhere to be seen. All they see is some blood, a hacksaw, his handcuffs and Merle's dismembered hand.

In the fourth episode, Rick's group try to find Merle but there's no sign of him. They go to get the guns but come under attack from a gang of Latino survivors. They attack Daryl and he shoots one of them in the backside. Glenn is taken prisoner. Rick and the others manage to capture one of the injured Latino fighters and find out where the others will have taken Glenn. They head there, hoping to do a straight swap – there's no way they're leaving Glenn behind.

The other group want more – they want their man and the guns. Things turn nasty but thankfully a woman steps in and calms them down. She is the grandmother of one of the men. It turns out that the men are putting on an act. The Latino group took over an old people's home after the staff fled and are determined to protect the old people even now.

They swap prisoners and Rick gives them some of the guns, but when they go to get their van they find it has gone. They think Merle must have taken it. They head back to the camp and arrive just in time. A large group of walkers has ventured up the hill and has taken the survivors by surprise; Ed and a woman called Amy have been killed. Rick, Glenn, T-Dog and Daryl help to kill the remaining walkers.

In the fifth episode, Amy's sister Andrea is struggling to cope with the fact that Amy is dead and she doesn't want to be separated from her sister's body. She has to, though, when Amy reanimates as a walker. Andrea has no choice but to kill her. During the battle, group member Jim was bitten and everyone knows it's only a matter of time before he too becomes a walker. They will do anything to stop that happening and decide to head for the CDC. Shane thinks there's no point but he's overruled.

One family decide not to travel with the main group and just want to try to survive on their own. They leave for their home of Birmingham, Alabama. The others set out for the CDC but during the journey Jim makes the decision that he wants to be left behind. He wants to be with his dead family. The others go on but when they get to the CDC building they think it is empty. As they turn to go Rick notices a camera and he knows that someone must be watching them. He speaks to the camera, asking for the group to be let in. The doors open...

The man in the CDC is Dr Edwin Jenner, who has been living and working on his own and had been considering suicide before Rick and the survivors arrived. His own virus test sample had gone and he didn't know what to do next.

In the dramatic climax to the series a flashback reveals that it was Shane who saved Rick's life. When the walkers attacked, Shane had tried to take Rick out of the hospital but couldn't because soldiers were forcing everyone out and the walkers were smashing their way in. He left, but before he did he blockaded Rick's door.

In the present day, the group try to enjoy being in the CDC building, enjoying the food and wine. Shane drinks too much and tries to explain to Lori that he had thought that Rick was dead – he hadn't been trying to deceive her. He tries to get close to her but she isn't interested and he pushes things too far. She manages to stop him before he forces himself on her.

The survivors ask Dr Jenner how people become walkers and he explains what happens to their brains and bodies. The group also learn that they have limited time in the building because it is set to self-destruct once the power supply runs out. A clock on the wall shows that will happen very shortly, and Dr Jenner thinks it is for the best. The others don't want to give up like him and want to get out. They manage to convince Dr Jenner to let them go but he stays behind; he is ready to die. He whispers something to Rick but the others can't make out what he says. Two of the group, Jacqui and Andrea, decide to stay behind but group member Dale manages to persuade Andrea to leave with them as he will stay and die with her otherwise.

As they make it outside, the building explodes, killing Dr Jenner and Jacqui. The remaining survivors drive off in their vehicles…

The end of the first series was very different from the comics, but co-creator Robert Kirkman didn't mind. He explained to A.V. Club: 'At the onset of the comic book series, I didn't know how long it would last – I didn't know if it'd get cancelled. So I was trying to get as many big ideas, as many stories in there as possible. But this is something I really pushed for the show: I came into the writers' room the first day and said: "Look, I don't care about the comic." I don't want people who've read the comic to be bored. Like Frank [Darabont, who developed the show and leads the writing team] came to me with the CDC storyline, and I was pretty much into anything that'll keep the show compelling.'

Six million people watched the finale in the US and the series received many nominations for top awards. It was put forward for Best New Series at the 2011 Writers Guild of America Awards and Best Television Series Drama at the Golden Globes. The show and cast were also nominated for six Saturn Awards – Best Television Presentation, Best Actor on Television (Andrew Lincoln), Best Actress on Television (Sarah Wayne Callies), Best Guest Starring Role on Television (Noah Emmerich), Best Supporting Actor on Television (Steven Yeun) and Best Supporting Actress on Television (Laurie Holden). The Directors Guild of America also nominated Frank Darabont for their Outstanding Directorial Achievement in a Dramatic Series Award for 'Days Gone By' (the pilot).

The second series will mean new characters, and fans will be excited to see who is cast as vet Hershel Greene, his daughter Maggie, and Otis, his farmhand. In the comics Hershel has a large family and keeps walkers in his barn. As well as Maggie, he has Shawn, Lacey, Arnold, Billy and twin girls Susie and Rachel. He just wants to protect his family and doesn't always agree with the things that Rick says. They have an argument and go their separate ways but Hershel later joins the group of survivors in their prison hideout and teaches them how to grow their own crops. He dies after his son Billy is killed but it's not known if he will meet the same fate in the TV series.

The people at AMC want the second series to be even better than the first. Robert Kirkman told *Entertainment Weekly*: 'We're mapping out everything. We got a lot of cool ideas. Everyone here is mindful of how well received the first season was. We're breaking our backs, story-wise, to make sure the next season is twice is good, or three times as good, with a lot of twists and turns and pushing the envelope of what you can do on TV... I know Frank [Darabont] has said we're going to see Hershel's farm. We're looking to take some picturesque rural landscapes and playing with that and coming up with some cool zombie visuals. We'll see some of the locations of the first season, but we're going to mainly focus on breaking new ground.'

Rick is played by British actor Andrew Lincoln (real name Andrew James Clutterbuck), who is best known in the UK for playing Simon in the sitcom *Teachers* and Mark in the romantic comedy *Love Actually*.

He found the scenes in the first episode where he had to ride his horse challenging because he's not a natural, but his wife, who is, thought he did really well. Rick was very fond of his horse Blaze until it was eaten by the walkers!

Andrew revealed to AMC that if he had to leave his life behind in a zombie apocalypse he would take swimming trunks, a tennis racket and a gun. He also admitted the food he would miss the most would be prosciutto ham.

Andrew's family moved to Atlanta while he was filming the first series but, because his children are young, he protected them from seeing the walkers. His daughter did catch a glimpse, however, as he explained to AMC: 'They're both quite young. My eldest is three years old. It's not the most kid-friendly set you would wish for. But in Atlanta there is a puppetry museum, so there are lots of Jim Henson puppets and there is a Big Bird there. They took a wrong turn one morning and went into the wrong trailer: It was Greg Nicotero and his team and they had this corpse that was rotting. My daughter just went up and started prodding it, and she seemed pretty cool about the whole thing. She said: "It's kind of like a Big Bird for grown-ups." That's the way she explained zombies.'

Shane is played by American actor Jon Bernthal. After spending some time as a professional baseball player, he learned his craft in the Moscow Art Theatre School. The vast majority of Jon's acting has been on the stage and he has performed in more than 30 plays. He has appeared as a character actor in numerous US TV series, including playing Duncan in the sitcom *The Class* and Sergeant Manuel 'Manny' Rodriguez in the TV mini-series *The Pacific*. His movie appearances include Al Capone in *Night at the Museum 2*.

He never expected to be playing one of the leading men in the show and would have been happy just being an extra. Asked by *SFX* if he read the original comics when he got the part of Shane, he replied: 'At first no, man. At first the way it works out here is there's something called pilot season, where all the new shows get a chance at being made, and it was kinda part of that. For a guy at my stage who's sort of at the beginning of his career, pilot season is a really important time.

'My agent sent me, like, 150 different scripts and I had read everything, and then when I read *The Walking Dead* I wrote a separate letter back to my agent just saying I would love to be… I'd be an extra in this thing! It was the best-written pilot I've ever read. I've never read anything that paid that kind of attention to detail in terms of atmosphere and character, it was just so rich and textured – such a wonderfully written script. I had no idea it was based on a comic. As the project went forward I began to look into the comic a little bit, but, y'know, Shane died so fast in that that I don't know how much it really helped!

'I think that in the show we've taken a different turn with Shane, much to Frank Darabont's credit – and to Robert Kirkman's, for not being overly precious with the material. They've really tried to make Shane a far more three-dimensional character in the show, and tried to flesh him out a little bit. I mean, for me it's great because I get to keep my job! But I also think it serves the story, and I'm really excited that they decided to go that way with it, because I love this show so much – I love being a part of it. But since then I've become a fan of the comic, I think it's great.'

If there were a real zombie apocalypse Jon reckons that he would have the best chance of surviving out of the actors who work on *The Walking Dead*. He told AMC TV: 'We're actors – we'd all pretty much suck, but I think I would suck the least.'

He also revealed which walker in series one he enjoyed killing the most. 'I liked Gale's daughter. Gale Anne Hurd is the executive producer and her daughter was there as we were coming out of the CDC. I got to shoot her right before she went off to Princeton, which is pretty cool. We were just like full-on sprint. Bam! Right in the head. And she fell great. The whole thing was kind of crazy. You're shooting your boss's daughter. It was insane!'

The leading lady in the show is Lori, played by Sarah Wayne Callies. After graduating from the prestigious Dartmouth College in New Hampshire, she took a Master of Fine Arts degree at Denver's National Theater Conservatory. She is best known for playing Dr Sara Tancredi in *Prison Break*.

Sarah particularly enjoyed shooting the scene where she sees Rick again. 'That was an interesting scene,' she told AMC TV. 'As opposed to most reunion scenes, the first thing that she feels when she sees him is horror, because the only possible explanation is that he's a walker. Shane said he died. The next thing that goes through her head is a different kind of horror, which is: Shane lied to me. This changes everything. As significant as the apocalypse is in changing her marriage, she only comes to find out after the fact she's committed infidelity.'

Sarah added that she loves working with the actors who play Rick and Shane. 'I get to do these things with Andy Lincoln and Jon Bernthal, and they are extraordinary men. The love triangle that exists between these people constantly reminds me of Camelot. You have Arthur, Guinevere and Lancelot. Which two of those three love each other more? Arthur and Lancelot may love each other more than either one of them love Guinevere. And they actually love each other so much and so unsustainably that they will destroy each other. There's no way this ends well. Let's do that. That's amazing.'

DID YOU KNOW?

It was Jon Bernthal's idea for Shane to wear his number 22 football jersey number around his neck. He also wears Shane's big police boots all the time, even though they are covered in fake blood.

WHITE ZOMBIE (1932)

White Zombie is said to be the first zombie horror film ever made. It was directed and produced by Victor Halperin and his brother Edward. The script was written by Garnett Weston and it took 11 days to shoot at a cost of $50,000, which was a phenomenal amount of money in those days. Béla Lugosi played Murder Legendre, Madge Bellamy played Madeleine Short Parker, John Harron played Neil Parker and Robert Frazer played Charles Beaumont. At the time of its release, reviewers felt that the cast weren't very good and the storyline was too exaggerated to be taken seriously. Nonetheless it has become a classic movie.

The film starts with Madeleine Short arriving in Haiti to be reunited with her fiancé Neil Parker. They are on their way to stay with rich plantation owner Charles Beaumont when they pass the evil voodoo witch doctor Murder Legendre. Unbeknown to the couple, Charles is completely infatuated with Madeleine and has turned to the witch doctor in the hope of luring Madeleine away from Neil and getting her to marry him instead. Murder Legendre tells Charles that the only way to get Madeleine is to convert her into a zombie, like Murder Legendre's horde of zombies. Charles agrees and convinces the couple to have their wedding on his plantation. Charles slips Madeleine a special potion that Murder Legendre gives him and during the wedding ceremony she dies.

After she has been buried, Murder Legendre and Charles break into her tomb and bring her back to life as a zombie. Neil has no idea and later the night, stricken with grief, he goes to his wife's tomb only to discover that she is no longer there. He doesn't know what to do and goes to speak to Haiti's missionary Dr Bruner. He suspects that Murder Legendre has turned her into a zombie, so together they travel to the witch doctor's castle. Meanwhile, Charles realises that zombie Madeleine isn't the woman he loved and wishes to change her back to human form, but Murder Legendre has other plans. He has been plotting all along to use Madeleine and he drugs Charles with the potion so he becomes a zombie too.

The witch doctor can sense that Neil and Dr Bruner have come to get him and orders the zombified Madeleine to kill her husband. She tries to attack Neil with a knife but Dr Bruner grabs her and she drops it. Murder Legendre then orders the rest of his zombies to kill Neil but Dr Bruner knocks Murder Legendre unconscious, which stops him from being able to control the zombies. The undead walk over a cliff and will never hurt anyone again. Murder Legendre wakes up and tries to escape but Charles pushes him off the cliff before falling over himself. With Murder Legendre dead, Madeleine becomes human again and can start her new life with Neil.

DID YOU KNOW?

Heavy metal band White Zombie named themselves after this movie.

X IS FOR...

THE X-FILES (1993–2002)

The hit sci-fi TV show *The X-Files* ran for almost 10 years. Created by Chris Carter, it follows the investigations of two FBI Special Agents, Fox Mulder (David Duchovny) and Dana Scully (Gillian Anderson). The show covered many aspects of the strange, scary and paranormal, with some episodes looking at cases involving zombies.

FRESH BONES (1995)

'Fresh Bones' was the 15th episode of the second series. Written by Howard Gordon and directed by Rob

Bowman, it sees Mulder and Scully investigating several murders in a Haitian refugee camp.

The episode starts with US Marine Jack McAlpin, who is stationed at the refugee compound. At home eating breakfast, McAlpin is startled to see that his cereal suddenly appears to turn into maggots! Shaken by what he sees, McAlpin runs from his house and drives off. In the car he looks in the mirror to see his face decomposing, as if he's turning into a corpse. This causes the frightened man to drive his car into a tree, apparently killing him. The camera pans out to reveal a veve (voodoo symbol) drawn on the tree.

It's believed in the camp that McAlpin's death is suicide, the second among soldiers in a short time, bringing Mulder and Scully to investigate. Although the veve on the tree wasn't seen by others, McAlpin's wife suspects voodoo is involved in her husband's death, having seen the same symbol in their backyard. At the camp the investigators meet its commander, Colonel Wharton, and an imprisoned refugee, Pierre Bauvais.

Things start getting strange when Mulder finds McAlpin's body missing at the morgue. Then the pair see the 'dead' soldier wandering down the middle of a road. When questioned, McAlpin explains that he doesn't recall his death. Testing reveals a chemical used in Haitian zombie ceremonies in the soldier's blood. This leads the investigators to the grave of the other dead soldier, where they find that the body is missing...

The pair are told that the camp commander has been beating the Haitian refugees following threats by Bauvais to take the souls of the soldiers if the Haitians are not allowed to return to their country. Following these allegations, Wharton has Bauvais beaten to death. Harry Dunham, another marine at the base, is then found dead, and Mulder catches McAlpin with a knife near the scene. He confesses to the murder, although again he was in a 'zombie' state with no recollection of the event.

When the agents find out that Dunham and the other dead soldier were planning to testify against the camp commander, they go to the cemetery to find the commander performing a voodoo ceremony over the dead refugee's grave. The episode ends with Wharton being buried alive and McAlpin revealing that one of the Haitians they'd met had actually died weeks earlier!

MILLENNIUM (1999)

Directed by Thomas J Wright, 'Millennium' was another episode to touch on the subject of zombies.

Set in Tallahassee, Florida, the episode starts at the memorial service for an ex-FBI agent, Brandon Crouch. At the service a man tells Crouch's widow that he once worked with her husband, and when everyone has left he places a mobile phone in the coffin… A week later it rings and the mysterious man heads to Crouch's grave.

Mulder and Scully are brought in to investigate the empty grave of the former agent. It's revealed this isn't the first time an FBI agent has committed suicide only to have their body exhumed from the grave. It's thought the whole thing has been staged, but damage to the inside of the coffin points to the body leaving from the inside, which suggests only one thing… zombies!

Following the evidence found, the pair are asked to investigate the Millennium Group. Made up of ex-FBI agents, the Millennium Group believe in a biblical prophecy at the start of the new millennium. Mulder and Scully are told by a former member that the strange cult believe they can bring about the end of the world by killing themselves before the millennium.

As the investigation progresses, reports are revealed of zombies rising from the dead in the hunt for victims. Scully is attacked at the morgue by the dead agent and Mulder is attacked by a group of living dead. Scully saves him by shooting them in the head, the only way they can be stopped. The intervention of Mulder and Scully stops the weird cult from bringing about the end of the world, and they end the episode ready for their next investigation.

DID YOU KNOW?

Scully shooting the zombies in the head near the end of the episode is a reference to the zombie classic *Night of the Living Dead*.

Y IS FOR...

YOROI: SAMURAI ZOMBIE (2008)

Directed by Tak Sakaguchi, *Yoroi* is a low-budget gore-fest that combines modern crime and gangsters with ancient samurai zombies.

The movie starts with a family on a trip. All is going well until they come across a car accident and pull over to help. The family's car ends up being hijacked by a pair of criminals on the run. With a gun pointed to his head, the father is forced to drive the fugitives. Taking a route through the woods to avoid a blockade, things start to turn from bad to worse as the car's satellite navigation screen turns blood red. Then the car suddenly breaks down, leaving the family stranded in the woods with the criminals.

The desperate criminals force the father to go and hunt for tools to get the car started, so he heads off into the distance, miles from anywhere. With no idea where he is, the father comes across a deserted village. He climbs to the highest point in the village, where he finds a cemetery. Then, for no apparent reason, he digs and finds a rusty knife, which he uses to cut off his own head!

In fact his actions are under the control of Yoroi, a zombie samurai, who guards the deserted village. The undead warrior then rises from his tomb and chops up the father's head in a blood-heavy gore scene. He then makes his way to the rest of the family...

Z IS FOR...

THE ZOMBIE DIARIES (2006)

A low-budget, independent British horror movie directed and written by Michael Bartlett and Kevin Gates, *The Zombie Diaries* was filmed as if it were a documentary. In the introduction two scientists are taking tissue from a zombie that has been shot while soldiers clear the nearby farmhouses.

The first diary of the movie, entitled 'The Outbreak', then starts. Londoners are aware that an unknown virus is spreading and a small crew are sent to investigate what is happening in the country. They come across some zombies...

The second diary of the movie is entitled 'The Scavengers' and occurs a month after the outbreak started. Three people are searching for supplies and carry one gun between them.

The third diary is entitled 'The Survivors' and shows how a group of people are managing to live on a farm together, fighting off any zombies that come too close. The group is made up of all kinds of people – they argue and fight each other at times. They are shown killing zombies but then the story goes back to the scenes in part one when the film crew arrive, and two crazed members of the survivor group kill everyone apart from one member of the crew. It wasn't the zombies but the psychopaths within the group that brought about their downfall.

Anton Bitel wrote in his review for the Eye For Film website: 'Here the rough-and-ready handheld video purports to be "found" footage shot on the fly by three different groups caught up in the disaster. Yet what at first seems a refreshing vérité take on the whole zombie genre soon imports problems of its own, as you find yourself wondering why these people do not just drop their cameras while they hide, run and (eventually, inevitably) die screaming.

'Like any self-respecting apocalyptic horror made in the post-9/11 era, *The Zombie Diaries* duly references the collapse of the Twin Towers, rural livestock culls and bird flu epidemics – but it has another, more covert agenda, slyly satirising the Noughties obsession with documenting any and every aspect of experience for public consumption. This is horror well and truly updated for the YouTube/reality TV generation.'

The reviewer for FEARnet.com wasn't too impressed with the movie but still found it had some good parts. 'The multi-plotted approach doesn't really work all that well, feeling more like an editorial room gimmick than an intentional story-telling device. Plus the fractured narrative works to slow the movie down to a crawl, and I doubt that's what co-directors Michael Bartlett and Kevin Gates were going for. Throw in some plot threads that are left dangling and a distractingly underdeveloped story arc, and sure (as is often the case when dealing with a low-budget genre film made by people with more enthusiasm than cash), there's plenty of nitpicks to make on *The Zombie Diaries*.

'But that's not to say that Bartlett and Gates don't have a few cool ideas or deliver a few solid sequences. The zombie attacks and the gore-droppings arrive on only an intermittent basis, but a solid handful of the shocks/scares work surprisingly well. And while the flick certainly doesn't need to offer a "one month earlier" subplot, some of the material found in this section is pretty grim and disturbing.'

ZOMBIELAND (2009)

A zombie comedy, *Zombieland* was directed by Ruben Fleischer, produced by Gavin Polone and taken from a screenplay scripted by Rhett Reese and Paul Wernick. On its release the movie received great reviews from critics and zombie fans, and took $60.8 million in its first three weeks alone.

The story is set in Texas two months after an outbreak of mad cow disease, which has mutated and turned millions of people into zombies. A shy student called Columbus (Jesse Eisenberg) is travelling to Ohio to see if his parents have survived but he crashes his car and is forced to walk. He meets someone called Tallahassee (Woody Harrelson) who is on a mission to find the last remaining Twinkies on the planet. (Twinkies are sponge cakes with a cream filling, mainly eaten in the USA.)

The pair decide to travel by car together but encounter a hilarious situation when they stop at a food store and meet two sisters called Wichita (Emma Stone) and Little Rock (Abigail Breslin). The girls manage to trick Columbus and Tallahassee into handing over their weapons and promptly steal their car. The boys eventually find another truck, filled with loads of weapons, to get them back on the road. Later they come across the girls again on the highway, and again they try to highjack the guys' truck and weapons. The four call a truce and decide to travel together.

The group then start planning where they should head. The girls say they want to go to Pacific Playland, a supposedly zombie-free amusement park in California, but Columbus protests, saying he wants to go to Ohio to find his parents. Wichita tells him that his hometown has been invaded by zombies so his parents are more than likely dead. After weighing this up they set out for Pacific Playland. On their way they stop in Hollywood where Tallahassee takes them to see Bill Murray at his mansion. Murray is dressed as a zombie in disguise and explains that this allows him to continue to live his old life and he can play golf without being attacked by real zombies. He pulls a prank on Tallahassee and Little Rock to scare them but, unfortunately for him, he is then shot by Columbus who thinks he is a real zombie.

Columbus believes Tallahassee is grieving for his dead dog, but as the group continue to bond in a somewhat dysfunctional manner, Columbus discovers that it was Tallahassee's son who was killed, not his dog. Wichita develops feelings for Columbus and nearly kisses him but then gets frightened. She takes Little Rock and leaves the boys, continuing on the quest to Pacific Playland. Columbus doesn't want them to go and persuades Tallahassee to come with him as he goes after the girls in one of Bill Murray's vehicles.

The sisters reach Pacific Playland and in their excitement turn on all the rides, rollercoasters and stalls.

Suddenly zombies swarm over the amusement park after being attracted by the lights and noise. The sisters are suddenly stuck, trapped on top of a ride with a drop tower, but in the nick of time Columbus and Tallahassee appear. Tallahassee manages to distract the majority of zombies away from them and then locks himself in a games booth and hides. Columbus saves the girls from imminent death. Wichita then reveals that her real name is Krista and they kiss.

In the closing scene Tallahassee kills the remaining zombies, and is rewarded by Little Rock who hands him a Twinkie she has found. The four then set out on another adventure as one small and slightly dysfunctional family.

Screenwriters Rhett and Paul had had the idea for *Zombieland* for four and a half years before they wrote the movie script. They had originally developed the idea into a script for a TV pilot and sold it to CMS in 2005. Rhett told FirstShowing.net: 'There is an executive at Sony Television, Chris Parnell, who had a ton of passion for it, and when it died as a television show, he and Gavin Polone, our producer, who also has a ton of passion for it, decided to try to convince Sony to allow us to, to pay us, to expand it into a back-door pilot or made-for-television movie, or maybe a straight-to-DVD movie.

'... episode two became the second half of the

movie. And so that was a blast, but when we were finished Gavin Polone got the script and he thought it was too expensive now and he also thought: "Maybe this is too good to be DVD – we should take it over to Sony Pictures" – which he did and they decided to make it.'

The movie's director Ruben Fleischer added in the location of the amusement park, and the names of some of the characters also changed. Columbus and Tallahassee were originally named Flagstaff and Albuquerque, and Little Rock was going to be called Still Water.

When they were casting the celebrity they wanted a 'zombified Patrick Swayze' making reference to his life and career, as well as dancing throughout his scenes for comedy value. Bill Murray was cast but other actors considered for the role included Matthew McConaughey, Kevin Bacon, Sylvester Stallone and Dwayne Johnson.

Rotten Tomatoes gave the movie a score of 90 out of 100 (based on 211 reviews) and said: 'Wickedly funny and featuring plenty of gore, *Zombieland* is proof that the zombie subgenre is far from dead.' Chris Hewitt from *Empire* magazine wrote in his review: 'Very funny, often thrilling and full of neat little touches that should make it entirely rewatchable, *Zombieland* sees Fleischer join the ranks of directors – Romero, Wright, Raimi, Snyder – whose first films aren't just zombie films, but great films.' Sam Bathe from Fan the Fire also loved the movie and said: '*Zombieland* will undoubtedly become the new zombie-comedy cult classic for the current generation.'

DID YOU KNOW?

Woody Harrelson set four conditions if he were to accept the role of Tallahassee. The first two were based on who was cast alongside him and the crew, and the third was that when making the film they were environmentally conscious. The fourth was that the director could not eat dairy products for a week. Ruben Fleischer found it hard at first but managed to do even better and became a vegan for almost a year.